John Bernard Dalgairns

The devotion to the heart of Jesus

With an introduction on the history of Jansenism

John Bernard Dalgairns

The devotion to the heart of Jesus
With an introduction on the history of Jansenism

ISBN/EAN: 9783744646772

Printed in Europe, USA, Canada, Australia, Japan

Cover: Foto ©Lupo / pixelio.de

More available books at **www.hansebooks.com**

The Devotion to
The Heart of Jesus.

THE DEVOTION TO The Heart of Jesus.

WITH

AN INTRODUCTION ON THE HISTORY OF JANSENISM.

BY

JOHN BERNARD DALGAIRNS,
Priest of the Oratory of St. Philip Neri.

NEW REVISED EDITION.

BALTIMORE:
PUBLISHED BY JOHN B. PIET,
LATE KELLY, PIET & CO.

Contents.

	PAGE
PREFACE TO THE AMERICAN EDITION	7
AUTHOR'S PREFACE	11

INTRODUCTION.
The Spirit of Jansenism 17

CHAPTER I.
History of the Devotion to the Sacred Heart 67

CHAPTER II.
The Adoration of the Sacred Heart 114

CHAPTER III.
The Love of the Heart of Jesus 152

CHAPTER IV.
The Love of the Heart of Jesus for Sinners 183

CHAPTER V.
The Love of the Heart of Jesus for those who are aiming at Perfection 217

CHAPTER VI.
The Heart of Jesus in the Blessed Sacrament 253

PREFACE TO THE AMERICAN EDITION.

THE work which is here presented to the American public is not a controversial treatise, but a doctrinal exposition of the devotion to the Sacred Heart of Jesus, now so extensively diffused throughout the Church. The author, a distinguished convert from the ranks of the Anglican clergy to the Catholic faith, was sensible that the subject of popular devotions is frequently obscure to the minds of those who have but recently become members of the Church; for, although they believe on her authority whatever is a matter of faith, they may not yet have acquired that intimate knowledge of her life and spirit which are exhibited in the practical and fruitful operation of her heaven-descended doctrines. To aid them in rightly apprehending the system of popular devotions is the object of the following pages. Though he treats more especially of the devotion to the Sacred Heart of Jesus, his remarks apply in general to all those which are approved by the Church, and show that they always spring legitimately from her theology, and that if they vary at different times, they are but various expressions or illustrations of her interior and unchanging life to meet the different phases of the world. These points, embracing the historical and dogmatical view of the devotion to the Sacred Heart of Jesus, are discussed in the first and second chapters; the remaining four treat of the love of that Divine Heart, or what may be termed the mystical grounds of the devotion. As an introduction to the subject, the author has given a very interesting sketch of the origin, progress, and spirit of Jansenism, the most fearful enemy of popular devotion in the last century.

This brief outline of the writer's plan, which he has executed with considerable ability, will suffice to show that his work will prove a source of valuable information, not only to converts, but to those also who have been reared in the belief of Catholic doctrine, by affording more ample instruction on a topic to which only a few words of explanation are commonly devoted in our manuals of piety. We may add that the author, in the performance of his task, has not disdained the ornaments of style. His language is polished, yet clear and vigorous, and breathes that devout fervor which he aims at enkindling in the hearts of his readers.

AUTHOR'S PREFACE.

AN apology seems due for publishing a work which is not purely devotional on the subject of the Sacred Heart. The object of it is by no means to supersede, but to act as an auxiliary to, books of devotion. It is certain that the system of popular devotions is often the last to work into the heart of a convert, even after his intellect has been convinced by the dogmas of the Church. To those who come out of a body in which acts of faith, hope, and charity are unknown, the value assigned to an act of love, and still more the affectionateness of God's ways of dealing with the soul implied in that system, must necessarily seem strange and startling. It was thought, therefore, not unprofitable to show how the devotions of the Catholic Church form an integral part of her history, and spring most naturally out of the most exact theology. It will be found, on examination, that the idea of Jesus, contained in Catholic hagiology, is precisely identical with that which is painfully gathered by the student from the Summa of St. Thomas, or the pages of Suarez and De Lugo. Nay, the author would think it no extravagance to assert that the primitive Church, which could believe the vision seen by St. Dionysius of Alexandria and the apparition of our Lady and St. John, to St. Gregory Thaumaturgus, had its own hagiology, and would have found nothing strange in the story of the appearance of our Lord to the Venerable Margaret Mary Alacoque.*

Though the present work is not strictly devotional, the author has felt so averse to introduce controversy into it that he has preferred to relegate to the preface even a passing notice of what might tend to provoke it. The question here raised, as to the cause of the wonderful spread of the devotion to the Sacred Heart, has been answered in a far different way from that proposed in this volume. Some of our readers may remember an article which appeared in the British Critic, for January, 1839, on the Revival of Jesuitism. When it is said that the writer of the article looks upon "Blair, in Scotland, Ushaw, near Durham," and even the harmless schools for female children of St. Aloysius, in Camden Town, as "Jesuit Colleges," and represents Maynooth as under Jesuit influence, the reader will be prepared for any amount of blunder, however preposterous. Yet the following astonishing sentiment will be far more than the utmost stretch of his imagination could have anticipated. Speaking of the rapid propagation of the devotion to the Sacred Heart, he puts and answers the following question: "If the visions of Sister Mary *Magdalen* are neither of divine relation, nor proposed as an article of divine faith, why have Popes and Princes, Italian stone-masons and Irish bricklayers, French Abbés and Prussian Bishops, cast their heads together to send them through the world? The plain truth may be

---

* Eusebius, Hist. vii. 7; St. Greg. Nyss. Op. ii. 977. V; also Bull. Defensio Fidei. 418.

read in letters of blood in more than one country in Europe." What the devotion to the Sacred Heart can have to do with bloodshed is indeed a mystery until the writer goes on to allude to revolutions, such as those of Belgium and of France, in 1830, and to civil wars, like that of Don Carlos, in Spain. From the context of the article, of which this sentence is the peroration, we gather that the reviewer considers that the Society of Jesus is the agent of all rebellions and political convulsions throughout the world, and, consequently, that Confraternities of the Sacred Heart, which he looks upon simply as Jesuit organs, are their secret political agents. In another place, in speaking of those associations, he asks, "Why must the names of every member be registered, and a report be remitted to Rome of each incorporated station?" The answer he puts in italics, "There was never yet such secret organization without conspiracy behind."

It is really hoped that the answer given in the following pages to the question will be more satisfactory, even to Protestants, than the wild solution of this fanatical writer. As for Catholics, and especially the members of the Confraternities, the astonishment with which they hear themselves looked upon as a species of European Ribbonmen, can only be equalled by the pity which they feel for a person laboring under such an extraordinary illusion. They will see in the words quoted above a fresh proof of the supernatural spread of the devotion, since it so struck the writer in question, that he could not account for it except by so astounding a supposition. Unhappily, it further reveals the melancholy fact that the Incarnation has so little hold upon his mind that he cannot possibly comprehend the Catholic doctrine on the adoration of the Sacred Humanity. It is for this that he accuses Catholics of giving "to the human substance which Jesus took from the Blessed Virgin the properties of His eternal nature." "Instead of adoring in the mystery of the Incarnation that fulness of the Godhead which united itself to the form of man," according to him we "give to the flesh and blood materially the heavenly virtue which belongs to the *spiritual part* of His being." The devotion to the Sacred Heart is a "debasing will-worship;" and he cites with wonder and disapprobation the notion which he has found in a Catholic writer, that, "in consequence of the hypostatical union, the heart of the King of kings is raised to an infinite dignity, which makes it worthy of our profound homage and adoration."

With such a slight appreciation of the doctrine of the Incarnation, it is not wonderful that the spread of the devotion to the Sacred Heart should be so incomprehensible to him that he is obliged to have recourse to the wildest hypothesis, in order to account for it. No wonder that it was a mystery to him why the whole Church, the Sovereign Pontiff, and the tonsured seminarist, Irish hodmen in the streets of London, and Italian peasants on the Apennines, queens of France, and savages in Canada, united to adore the Heart of Jesus, since the very principles which have guided Catholic theology in the adoration of the Sacred Humanity, from the Council of Ephesus down to the bull Auctorem Fidei, are utterly unknown to him. The heathen emperors also suspected a conspiracy, because they saw in Christianity an association, the moving spirit of which was hidden from them.

The devotion to the Sacred Heart has a principle of propagation within itself utterly independent of the particular instruments employed to spread it; and that principle is the love of Jesus, God and man. The reviewer ought to have remembered that the very universality of the devotion, at a time when the Society of Jesus was suppressed, is a plain proof that it had a momentum of its own, since it still progressed even after those who were principally concerned in promoting it were withdrawn. It is quite true that, even after the suppression, the Society had still those who most naturally regretted, and most deservedly admired it; yet they were but a portion of the Church. The ubiquitous existence of the Confraternities cannot be ascribed to such a cause as this, since it went on at a time when the very fact of the suppression proves that the admirers of the Society were by no means the whole Catholic world, nor the most powerful party within it. The propagation continued through means, and in places, utterly beyond Jesuit influence. One fact alone will show this. A French Bishop issued a mandate in favor of the Sacred Heart. In a book* which accompanied this document, he declares that the opponents of the devotion had confidently expected that Clement XIV. would cease to favor its propagation. He, on the contrary, cites a brief of indulgences granted by that Pontiff, in 1773, to a Confraternity erected in his own Cathedral, declares that he obtained it without difficulty, and vouches that he himself knew of several others accorded under the same circumstances. If any refutation of the reviewer were

---

* Le Culte de l'Amour Divin, by De Fumel, Bishop of Lodève.

needed, this is a most complete proof of the unsoundness of the very foundation on which he has built so monstrous an edifice.

It only remains to be added that the following pages contain the substance of two sets of lectures, one delivered in the chapel of the London Oratory, the other in the Church of St. Mary's, Moorfields.

If they should contribute to do away in some measure, with strong prejudices against Catholic devotions, or to increase but one degree higher the love of Jesus in the heart of any of the children of the Church, the author will feel that God has blessed them far above their deserts.

The Oratory, Birmingham,
    The Feast of St. Edmund, Confessor, 1852.

INTRODUCTION.

THE SPIRIT OF JANSENISM.

Besides the great acts of adoration and sacrifice ordered by our Lord, and bound up with the very existence of the Church, there is a body of devotions, authorized more or less directly by her, and taken up at different times with various degrees of enthusiasm by the faithful. In the following pages it is shown, by the example of one of these particular devotions, that the spread of them is not the mere result of an irregular outburst of natural feeling, but follows a law, and is an integral part of the dealings of God with his Church. They are the means by which the Holy Spirit stirs up the stagnant waters of devotion in Christendom; they are the method by which the most abstruse doctrines of the Church find their way into the souls of the multitude, and exercise a living action upon them. These devotions are the produce of the heart of the Church, while dogmas are shaped by her intellect. All this is obvious enough to a Catholic; he enters spontaneously into confraternities, as his devotion leads him, knowing that they are authorized by the Holy See, from the fact that indulgences are attached to them; and he never philosophizes upon a system which is too obviously sanctioned by his heart to be judged by his reason. He may suspect that it is superfluous labor to show, as it is done in the following pages, that the principles on which these devotions are based lie deep in Christian theology. On the other hand, to the mind of those who are disposed to reason on the subject, one link may appear to be wanting to the evidence brought forward to show the importance of these devotions. It may be said that there is nothing wonderful, nothing supernatural in the spread of them among the faithful, since the multitude ever feels more than it reasons. It may be argued that it is exaggerating the importance of them to exact of all Christians, to be enthusiastic about the system, to believe in the power of them with God, or to feel in his own heart a peculiar attraction to any one of them. But, on the other hand, if it can be shown that these devotions have been the object of the peculiar hatred of heretics, this is quite sufficient in itself to destroy all notion of fancifulness in those who maintain their importance. The instinct of heresy is perfectly unerring; the demoniacs shrieked as Jesus approached, because the spirits which possessed them recognised in him something more than man; and

Jansenism would never have opposed the Sacred Heart, as it did, if it were not that it felt within the devotion, a power which it dreaded. Men never bestow the dignity of hatred on what is too insignificant for any thing but contempt. It will be well, in order to confirm this statement, to show the extent of the opposition made to this devotion, and to lay bare its secret causes, by an account of the great heresy which attempted to put it down. It will conduce to the glory of the Sacred Heart to show that for many years it was the watchword of the Church against error, nay, that it even had its martyrs.

To any one who examines into the history of Jansenism, few things are more inexplicable than the wonderful hold which it kept upon the public mind in France during so long a space of time. It was in the year 1640, that the Augustinus of Jansenius made its appearance, and the party which supported the doctrines contained in that work, was strong enough in 1789 to destroy the Catholic hierarchy of France, and to set up the constitutional clergy in its stead. And during this long career Jansenism managed to excite the enthusiasm of characters the most opposite, and to arm in its defence talents the most various. What could be the mighty charm which could bewitch at once the gloomy profundity of Pascal and the amiable brilliancy of Madame de Sévigné, which could inspire the Esther of Racine and the Satires of Boileau? Nay, a zeal for Jansenism spread beyond the boundaries of France; so ardently did it burn in the breast of Joseph II. that he staked in its defence the fair provinces of the Netherlands, and lost them in the obstinate attempt to carry out the views of the party against the Catholic prejudices of a brave people; while, at one and the same time, the Holy See was in dread lest France, Austria, and Naples should be lost to the Catholic Church, so powerfully did the doctrines contained in that folio stir up the minds of men. Strange, indeed, that an exotic system, born in the University of Louvain, the posthumous labor of a foreign doctor who won his bishopric as a reward for a libel* on the French nation, should thus fasten itself on the affections and the intellects of some of the noblest and greatest of the sons of France What was the marvellous attraction in these doctrines, that they exercised an influence so wonderful and so sustained on successive generations? Turn to the opinion of Jansenius themselves, and you will be still more at a loss to account for the fact. What was there so peculiarly attractive in the five propositions that they stirred up the zeal of half civilized Europe? The system which they embodied was precisely of that class which is popularly comprehended under the wide term of Calvanism among

---

* The Mars Gallicus, of which Jansenius was the author.

us. The author affirmed that our dear and blessed Redeemer did not die upon the cross for all men, but only for the predestinate; that the rest of mankind did not even receive from God sufficient grace to avoid mortal sin, while the just, who were ultimately saved, had a grace conferred upon them which reduced them to mere machines, since it necessitated their wills, and deprived them of the power of resistance. Most miserable and unattractive system! It takes away from God all the long-suffering and compassion with which his grace pleads with a sinner to the very last; it converts our most loving Creator into an arbitrary tyrant, imposing upon man laws too severe for his weak nature, without giving him supernatural power to fulfil them. It takes away from the very tenderness of Jesus on the cross, and destroys the gracefulness of his passion, since it holds that He, by a distinct act, marred the all-sufficiency of his sufferings, by refusing to offer them up for more than a chosen few. How it would paralyze all our efforts, if, when, as trembling sinners, we come to the feet of Jesus, we could not feel sure that He shed his precious blood for us! Our dying lips could not even kiss the crucifix except under a condition. Such is a popular but a perfectly true account of the doctrines of the Augustinus. Surely, if these are the opinions after which Europe went mad, the infatuation is even more unaccountable still. The very enumeration of them is a proof that the strength of Jansen ism could not lie there.

The fact is, that heresy has its spirit as well as its letter: its doctrines are really loved, cared for, and understood by few, but its spirit of resistance to a living authority is sure to gather a party around it. Let it but dexterously keep out of sight its most offensive doctrines, and contrive not to be cast out of the Church, it is sure to become the representative of interests and of principles of action quite apart from its theories, and thus to gain a strength which is not its own. Little did the ministers of Joseph know about the ponderous tome which was mouldering in the imperial library, while they strenuously defended Quesnel who had reproduced it in another shape: they only understood that the bull Unigenitus had emanated from Rome, and that the Jansenists would go all lengths in favor of the civil power against the Church.

Jansenism was a planned, systematic conspiracy against Rome, but not in the same sense as that of Luther and Calvin. Geneva and Augsburg waged an open war, Jansenism was a secret plot. Its strength did not lie in its doctrines, but in the terrible tenacity with which its disciples clung to them, and the no less terrible obstinacy with which they determined to remain within the visible communion of the Church of God, for the very purpose of eating into its vitals and braving its decrees. It was a uicidal act in Calvin to let himself be driven out of the Catholic Church, and to erect a Church in opposition to it. The clear good sense of the French nation had seen through the absurdity of men setting up for themselves in religion, and pretending to extract from the Bible, with a certainty unerring, yet not infallible, the pure and genuine faith of Jesus. Accordingly, Henry IV., after having fought his way to the throne of France, felt that he could not be its genuine king while he remained a Huguenot; and the fall of La Rochelle proclaimed, forever, that Protestant power was at an end, at the moment that the Augustinus was working in the brain of Jansenius, and the plot was ripening in the restless mind of St. Cyran.

In all this there is nothing new in the history of the Church: that Calvin should have his Jansenius, is not more wonderful than that Monothelites should follow Eutychians; the courtly and decorous Eusebius was not more different from Arius than Henri Arnauld of Angers, or Caulet of Pamiers was from the heresiarch of Geneva. The system of the Augustinus had little that was novel in it: Baius had held cognate doctrines, and had been condemned a short time before in the same university. What was new about it was the assumed reverence for tradition, the hurt tone of injured innocence with which the accusation of novelty was repelled, the systematic appeal to the ancient Church, and the proud assumption that it, and it alone, represented St. Augustine. Many a heresy has appealed to the primitive fathers against the present, living Spouse of Christ, but this appeal was the very formality of Jansenism. It animated all its policy. For nearly two centuries they clung sternly on to the Church which condemned them, appealing from the living to the dead. Condemnation after condemnation of their doctrines emanated from the Holy See, and still they kept their hold. Each time some miserable evasion served them as an excuse for remaining within the bosom of the Church, without renouncing the right to believe what she had condemned as contrary to the faith. Each time the drift of the evasion was, in some shape or other, to assert a principle which put it beyond the possibility of the Catholic Church to decide upon successive controversies as they arose. In other words, they denied the perpetual infallibility of the Church—what they conceded to the Church of the fifth century, they denied to that of the seventeenth. Their last subterfuge was a distinct affirmation of the principle, that to be a good Catholic, it was sufficient to receive the decisions of the Church with a respectful silence, without in the least submitting the interior judgment to what she had decreed. In other words, they affirmed the right to hold, as distinct from teaching, doctrines condemned by the successor of St. Peter.

That there was from the first a conscious plot to form a party within the Catholic Church, and to overwhelm her, there is abundant evidence to prove, without having recourse to the common story of a set meeting at Bourg-Fontaine, to organize it. The story, that six chiefs of the party assembled to concert measures for the propagation of Deism, refutes itself; for, whatever Jansenius and St. Cyran were, they were not Deists. The imprudent assertion could only lay the defenders of the Church open to the indignant sarcasms of Pascal. But that there was at the very outset of the existence of Jansenism a dishonest scheme of remaining within the Church to alter her whole discipline, and to thrust upon her doctrines which were not hers, is sufficiently plain. Before the publication of the Augustinus, before what was called Jansenism existed, the eagle eye of Richelieu had been fixed on St. Cyran; and the future heresiarch had been lodged in Vincennes. The act may have been arbitrary, but there was abundant evidence of a conspiracy against the Church, in the huge collection of manuscripts, enough, we are told, to fill forty volumes folio, found in his cabinet. When entreated to release St. Cyran from his prison, Richelieu answered, "If Luther and Calvin had been dealt with as I have dealt with St. Cyran, France and Germany would have been spared the torrents of blood which have inundated them for fifty years." This, be it observed, was several years before the Augustinus saw the light.

A more unexceptionable witness than Richelieu can be produced. St. Cyran was accused of attempting to form a new sect. The principal evidence on which he was sent to Vincennes, was that of St. Vincent of Paul. They had once been friends, and had ceased to be so. It turned out that he had tried to attach the saint to his party, and had been repelled. In one of St. Vincent's letters the following passage occurs: "St. Cyran one day spoke as follows to me: 'God has given, and still gives me great lights: He has shown me that, for the last five or six hundred years, there is no such thing as a Church. Before that time the Church was like a mighty stream with translucent waters. But now, what looks like the church, is nothing but a collection of mud. The bed of the river is the same; the waters are not what they were.' I said to him," continues the saint, "that all heresiarchs had made use of this pretext to establish their errors, and I cited Calvin as an instance. 'Calvin,' was his reply, 'has not been wrong in all his views; he has only erred in his method of defending them.'" From that hour, St Cyran and the saint ceased to be friends, and St. Vincent was the principal witness against him when he was imprisoned at Vincennes.

Richelieu, prompt as he was, in this case was too

late; St. Cyran's party had been already formed, and its most important acquisitions made before he was consigned to his prison. He had bound to himself a few devoted followers, and it appeared on his examination, that his usual parting words to those whom he directed were: Occulte, propter metum Judæorum. What these designs were, was plain enough from the result; the Church of God authorizes the system by which a Christian places himself under the direction of a particular priest, by whose advice he is guided in his spiritual life. Thus the obedience which in the cloister is exercised under a vow, is meritoriously practised, as far as can be, by persons living in the world. It is not a dogma of the Church, but it is something more than an opinion, authorized by the common practice of Christians, that no perfection is possible without direction. The dealings of God with the soul are reduced to a science by spiritual writers, and out of this science are framed certain rules, according to which directors guide the souls committed to their care. Great as is the difficulty of applying these rules in practice, still they are not arbitrary; but above all, they require for their due exercise perfect disinterestedness, humility, and singleness of purpose. It was this great trust which no priest should undertake without a call from God, or should wield without trembling, that St. Cyran determined to use for his own purposes, and to betray. His aim was especially to attach to himself men of talent and young ecclesiastics, and to employ them in education and in literary works. In this way he hoped by degrees to leaven the nation and the Church with the new opinions. Is it not plain that the idea was suggested by the wonderful success of the illustrious Society of Jesus, with this difference, —that the direction of souls, and the education of youth, which no one has ever dared to say that the Jesuits exercised except with a view to the glory of the Church, St. Cyran undertook for the purpose of undermining that very Church from which he derived his authority, and whose were the souls whom he took under his guidance?

Before his imprisonment, St. Cyran had already succeeded in attaching a number of men of talent to himself. Every one knows the wonderful outburst of devotion which took place in France in the seventeenth century. It was the period when St. Vincent of Paul might be seen familiarly treading the streets of Paris, and when M. Olier was one of its parish priests; numbers of nobleman and ladies in court and camp were leading lives of extraordinary perfection; while, up and down the obscure cloisters of the country, many a nun was living in a state of supernatural union with God. To and fro in the midst of this religious enthusiasm went St. Cyran, gifted with extraordinary powers of obtaining influence with a well-merited reputation for learning and powers of mind, and an undeserved one for sanctity. He made an attempt on St. Vincent of Paul, and wrote to Jansenius that he had great hopes of Cardinal de Berulle; and if the saintly instinct of these two great men was too much for him, still he succeeded in attaching to himself many devoted and ardent souls. Even at that early period he had allured Singlin from St. Vincent; Lancelot was detached from the community of St. Nicholas-du-Chardonnet; and the French Oratory lost its great preacher, Desmares. But the greatest success which St. Cyran obtained, was the hold which he had gained on the family of Arnauld. Before he had seen the inside of the prison at Vincennes he had already made a conquest which enabled him to set Richelieu's power at defiance.

There was an ancient abbey of the Cistercian Order not far from Paris which had been restored to its original strictness under circumstances the most unpromising. Marie Angélique Arnauld, when but a child, had received the Abbacy as a gift from its royal patron, according to a custom condemned by the Council of Trent, yet too prevalent at the beginning of the seventeenth century. But the grace of God touched the heart of the young abbess, and with a wonderful energy and strength of will she reformed the laxity which had taken the place of the old rule of St. Benedict, and established religious observance and regular cloister. The nuns under her rule threw aside their worldly dress, and resumed the white habit of St. Bernard, and the old arches of the abbey of Port Royal echoed again to the chanting of the ecclesiastical office instead of the profane songs and merriment of seculars. The reform bid fair to spread far and wide; the regal abbey of Maubuisson received the reform of Port Royal at the hands of Marie Angélique, and the world was astonished by the unparalleled modesty, with which the instrument of the good work renounced the crosier of the rich Abbacy when her work was done, and returned to the low, damp valley of Port Royal, where the conventual buildings were often hidden by the unhealthy exhalations from its undrained waters.

Now that we have before us the whole of the history of Port Royal, it is impossible not to feel a sort of melancholy when we read the pathetic letters addressed by the Mère Angélique to her director, St. Francis of Sales, consulting him about resigning even her poor abbey, from a wish to cease to be Superioress, and entreating him to take upon him the entire guidance of her soul. The answers of the Saint show at once his affection for her, and his full appreciation of her earnestness and energy, as well as of her restles and domineering spirit. Of all women in France, the Abbess of Port Royal required a director. She was like Madame de Chantal in some of the circumstances of her life, but she seemed destined to a work more resembling that of St. Theresa. Like the former, she was sprung of one of those families of France in which the profession of the law and the administration of justice was hereditary. As Madame de Chantal passed over the body of her son on her way from the world to the Order of the Visitation, in spite of the tears which the effort cost her, so the Abbess Angélique, in re-establishing the cloister at Port Royal, had to bar out her father, her mother, and her brother, and then fell back fainting in the parlour behind the grating. But on the other hand, like St. Theresa, she had to inspire new vigor and animation into an Order which had lost its fervor. She had to battle with lax confessors, after having won over refractory nuns. After having gained a signal victory, the despotic ruler of that little world felt, as she grasped her independent crosier, that she had that within her which required taming in its turn. The masculine mind and the unbending strength of will, before which her own nuns and the authorities of the Order had been forced to yield, had need of a rule, firm and gentle as that of the sweet St. Francis, to reduce its wild energies under the obedience of Christ. Well would it have been for her if she had left her abbey and had become, as she seems to have desired, a humble disciple of St. Jane Frances de Chantal. For some wise reasons of his own, the saintly Bishop of Geneva would never receive her into the Order of the Visitation, and he was called to his rest, leaving her still upon earth Abbess of Port Royal.

In an evil hour she fell under St. Cyran's direction, and from that moment the whole energy of that indomitable will was bent on promoting the cause of heresy. It is impossible not to mourn over her fate. Instead of being, what she might have been, a great instrument in the hands of God, she sunk into the tool of a miserable faction. She wasted her great energies in the impossible task of keeping within the Church without being thoroughly of it. She fell a victim to theories about the Fathers and primitive antiquity. She believed in the infallibility of St. Augustine instead of in that of the ever-living Church of God; nay, with all a woman's weakness, she staked this world and the world to come on Jansenius' view of St. Augustine. Who knows, however, whether she may not have been more deceived than deceiving? She seems to have clung on to the last to the hope that the Church would not be against her, and she died of a broken heart when an unequivocal order from the assembly of the French Church to sign the formulary brought the question to an issue.*

Her death, however, could not undo the evil which she had done in her lifetime. Not only did she

---

* August 6, 1661.

bring over her Abbey to the cause of Jansenism, but her family too; and to this may, in a great measure, be attributed the success of the party. The family of Arnauld was a host in itself. Arnauld d'Andilly, the brother of the Mére Angélique, when he retired to the solitude of Port Royal, made no sacrifice of family affections. Six sisters and five of his daughters were nuns in the Abbey, and two of his sons, as well as five nephews, had already quitted the world, and were living an ascetic life in the valley under its jurisdiction. It is impossible to overestimate the greatness of this acquisition to the cause of Jansenism. It was an indication, which the history of the party never belied, that it would have on its side one great political power in the realm,—that of the Parliaments. The Abbess Marie Angélique belonged to one of the great legal families of France,—to the *noblesse de la robe*. Her father was one of that race of bold lawyers who were equally ready to plead a cause and to levy a regiment of musqueteers against the League. Her grandfather had once been a Protestant, and had narrowly escaped with his life on the day of the massacre of St. Bartholomew. Afterward he became a Catholic, but he left as a baneful inheritance to his family the principles of parliamentary Gallicanism in their worst form. He was thus a fitting type of the spirit of the parliaments of France. Those great legal bodies of the realm were ever distinguished for their hatred of Rome. Sprung as they were from the monarch who dragged Boniface VIII. from Anagni, they ever showed signs of this original sin of their existence. Such a party was glad enough to have a faction within the Church to help them, and they were ever in the strictest league with the Jansenists as soon as the death of Louis XIV. left them to their natural instincts. The parliaments of France, as is well known, in no way resembled that of England; they were supreme courts of justice. They did not, except by accident, represent either the aristocracy of the realm or the majesty of the people; they represented directly only the law of France. Now the flower of the advocates of the parliament of Paris astounded the French bar by entering the solitude of Port Royal Around the Abbey, and on the ground under its jurisdiction, St. Cyran had conceived the idea of collecting a number of men to be occupied in literary works, and in the education of youth, as the nuns were to be employed in bringing up young ladies. The nucleus of these ascetics, or solitaries as they were most unfortunately termed, was the eloquent Le Maitre, the son of the Mère Angélique's sister, the first barrister of France. A number of other distinguished men collected together at Port Royal; but while the Briareus of Jansenism had a hundred arms, that which animated the heart of the party,— its strong, hard heart,—was the blood of the Arnaulds. All the while that the party was in its strength, an Arnauld governed it; the diplomatic rule of the wily courtier D'Andilly succeeded to St. Cyran's sway; then his nephew, Antony, the great Arnauld, as he was called, infused into it the gall and the talent of his controversial mind; while simultaneously a whole dynasty of the name governed the Abbey of Port Royal.

It was owing to these men that the Abbey acquired a world-wide name at the expense of the holiness of its inmates. Its solitude became peopled; it was to that lowly valley that men repaired whose names are identified with the best days of French literature. They left the world to pray, to be with God, to fast, and to turn Port Royal into a new Thebaid; but no fasting or austerities could tame the fiery spirits who congregated there. Never was man served like St. Cyran, nay, it is not often that God is served so faithfully and well, except by His saints. Even after he was dead, his idea was carried on after him. It was his plan thoroughly to get hold of the literature of his country, and to identify the triumphs of its language with the progress of his heresy. The energy, the clearness, and distinctness, the limpid transparency which pleases even when it has no depth, which can say any thing, and say it well, notwithstanding its poverty of words, the vivacity and power which have made the tongue of France the language of Europe, and the interpreter of the thoughts of all nations—all this was to be turned into the vehicle of Jansenism. And he succeeded. It was then that works were planned and executed which will live as long as the French language lives. The power of writing memoirs, so peculiar to the French, has been so well employed by them, that even at this distance of time, we could fancy that we are personally acquainted with those whom the Nécrologe of Port Royal registers as having gone to their graves. But upon all this there was one deep, dark stain, which it is wonderful that even the world should have forgotten—the stain of dishonesty. Who, in looking at the pictures of the quiet-looking nuns, sitting in a circle, spinning under the shadow of the trees in the convent-garden, would suspect for a moment the fierce sectarian spirit that was lurking in their breasts? All at once the reader is surprised, as the memoirs go on, to find that ecclesiastical superiors come among them, and try violently, as it appears, to force them to sign documents and formularies. Our sympathies are enlisted on their side, because the fact that the convent was the centre of rebellion has been dexterously kept concealed. The nuns refused their adhesion to the doctrines of the Church, on the ground that the questions in dispute were, as they urged, too deep for them. Surely, if they were what, be it remembered, they strenuously asserted, loyal children of the Catholic Church, it would have sufficed for them to adhere to doctrines which emanated from her, if it were only as youths sign the Thirty-nine Articles on entering an English university, without understanding them. But the fact notoriously was, that they did understand perfectly what was going on, and that Arnauld's book on frequent communion, and the other writings of the party, were perfectly familiar to them. Even at this distance of time, though not one stone is left upon another, our imagination can reproduce, without effort, the plan of the Abbey, the valley under its jurisdiction, its streams and fish-ponds; and who, on looking down from the heights above on its peaceful conventual buildings, its cloistered quadrangles, and the modest spire of its church, would suspect for a moment that he was standing on the crater of a volcano? Yet the solitaries who dwelt in that valley were in league with the machinations of the Fronde. If there are barricades in the streets of Paris, and fighting about the Palais Royal, the Duke de Luynes, a Jansenist, is a member of the upper council of the rebels, and the Chevalier de Sévigné, another Jansenist, commands the regiment levied by De Retz. The coadjutor himself, the wild and turbid spirit, whom his own confessions have revealed to us, while he was evoking from the alleys and hovels of Paris the haggard artisans, whose descendants in the great Revolution travelled the road to Versailles with pike and gun,—De Retz himself was in league with Port Royal. During the tumult it is said that there was as much hurrying to and fro between Paris and the Thebaid of the solitaries, as on the high road between the capital and a royal residence in a time of war.* Nor can the utmost charity suppose them to have been ignorant, as were many others, of De Retz's character, when his very paramour, the Princess de Guémené, when he was as yet only Abbé de Gondi, was the friend of Arnauld d'Andilly, and oscillated between Port Royal and the scene of her guilt.†

The same dishonorable spirit marked the whole policy of the party. They carried into theology the spirit of lawyers, and of dishonest ones too. They fought the whole battle with Rome by a series of quibbles of which a respectable attorney would be ashamed. And while this disgraceful contest was going on, and consciences were perplexed and tortured by it, the solitaries did not disdain machinations of other sorts in other places. There were intrigues up the back-stairs of palaces, and courtiers in the halls of the Tuilleries executed schemes which had been planned in the solitude of Port Royal. When Fouquet, the minister of finance, fell, mysterious relations between him and Port Royal were discovered. In 1671, with all his hatred

---

* Notice sur Port Royal, p. 81.
† Memoirs of De Retz, vol. i. 25.

of the sect, Louis XIV. was surprised into choosing an Arnauld as the colleague of Colbert and Louvois, and the triumph of the party was sealed by the reappearance of D'Andilly at Versailles; he quitted the solitude of Port Royal to turn courtier a second time, and to thank his sovereign for the honor done to his son.

So contagious was this dishonest spirit in Port Royal, that it seemed to infect all who came within the influence of the place. If there was one man more than another whose rectitude of purpose and independence of mind would have defended him from it, that man was Pascal. The mind, which in its ardent search after truth, had broken down maxims of physical science as old as philosophy itself, might have been supposed to be safe from the dishonesty, if not from the arrogance of the party. At first, the ardent speculations of his intellect, and the fits of gloom which came over him, disposed him to the Predestinarian views of Jansenius; but the world on the other hand had its charms for him, and the young philosopher hesitated long between Port Royal and the brilliant society of Paris. But an accident, which nearly cost him his life, threw him into a fresh state of gloom, and a fanatical love for Port Royal took possession of his soul. There are few things which we can less easily forgive Jansenism than the noble souls which it spoiled and corrupted; and the noblest mind which it overthrew was Pas cal's. The discoverer of the cycloid was turned into the fanatic who saw precipices open beneath his feet when he walked. He dreamed dreams, and believed them to be visions; they were such that any director in the Church would have pronounced them to be illusions, of which a devout girl would have been ashamed, yet his sickly imagination clung to them with as much devotion as that with which the wildest Wesleyan ever noted down the day, the hour, and the minute of his conversion. He wrote an account of them, and wore the paper round his neck like an amulet, and the royal library of Paris possessed, and probably possesses to this day, this melancholy witness of the wreck which Jansenism had helped to cause in that wonderful intellect. It was owing to Jansenism that his great work on the Evidences of Christianity should be nothing but a gigantic wreck, the very ruins of which show by their colossal proportions how magnificent the complete edifice would have been. Instead of it we possess the Provinciales. Happily for the reputation of their author, the learning of those letters was not his own; he is not, therefore, answerable for misquotations, mutilated passages, and suppression of context. But he is answerable for the disingenuousness of the whole line of defence. The genius of Pascal alone could have adorned the barren subject as it did, and have succeeded in interesting the world in a dispute which hitherto had been wrapped up in the terms of scholastic theology. He alone could have appealed from the tribunal of the Sorbonne to that of public opinion, and thrown the mysteries of grace on the discussion of the multitude. If any one then was bound to be honest, surely it was he who had undertaken to be the interpreter between the schools and the world; and when, throughout the length and breadth of France, the Provinciales were devoured, and the dogmas of the Church were flung on the wild waves of public opinion, surely the world had a right to suppose that their masculine eloquence and the limpid perspicuity of their style was a vehicle of truth. Nevertheless, in their very outset, he betrays the trust reposed in him. Instead of explaining what the heresy was, he denies its existence; he treats it as a phantom raised by the Jesuits. Instead of grappling with the question fairly, as one which involved the very foundations of the mysterious doctrine of grace, he represents it as a mere squabble of the schools, and reduces it to a simple question of fact, whether the famous five propositions were really contained in Jansenius. The world knows now how to appreciate such reasoning as this. It was a wretched quibble, unworthy of Pascal, thus to characterize a question, which really involved the profoundest metaphysical speculation on the nature of the human will. No one pretended that the five propositions were word for word in Jansenius; and it was an insult to the intellect, as well as the authority of the Church, on the part of men who pretended to be her children, to bind her down to the simple question, whether these five sentences were verbally there or no. The Augustinus is now forgotten or unread; but the testimony of men of the most opposite parties, of Bossuet and of Fenelon, proves that Cornet, in reducing the ponderous tome of these five propositions, had faithfully performed his task and really extracted its essence. With the light which a whole century, since Pascal's time, has thrown upon Jansenism, the most ingenious arguments to prove its non-existence would indeed be urged in vain.

But it did not always require the light of the future to destroy the effect of Pascal's indignant eloquence. He concealed the point at issue when he appealed* to the works of Arnauld on the Holy Eucharist, and to the perpetual adoration established at Port Royal, as a proof that Jansenists beliveed in Transubstantiation. No one doubts that they accepted all the doctrines of the Church on the subject of the Blessed Sacrament; but this did not exempt them from the charge of a revolt against her authority, since at the same time they rebelled against her discipline. The state of the community to which he appealed, was the best proof that could be desired

---

* Provinciales, Lettre 16.

that the spirit of Jansenism was rebellion against the present living Church of God. Enter the Abbey of Port Royal, and you would see, it is true, the Blessed Sacrament enthroned on high. A red cross on the white scapular of St. Bernard announced in the very habit of the nuns that the perpetual adoration had been added to their rule. But in the heart, which beat under that habit, was rooted a spirit of rebellion against the discipline of the Church, proud as that of Calvin against its doctrines. Pascal knew well when he wrote those lines that the adoration itself was a remnant of a former state of things, when the Abbey was under the direction of Zamet, Bishop of Langres, before St. Cyran had set his foot in it. The Jansenist displaced him: and though the nuns continued to adore our Lord, set up on high, far above them, as their king, they obstinately set their faces against that more intimate union by which He gives Himself frequently to Christians in the Holy Eucharist.

It was a fatal moment for Port Royal when Marie Angélique ceased to be under the direction of St. Francis of Sales: henceforth it became a monument of the danger of souls which set themselves in opposition to the devotional movement of the present living Church, to pursue the ideal standard of ages that are passed away. There were two systems at that time in France contending for the mastery. A spirit of love had risen up in the holy city of

Rome, announcing to men that their Lord would have them receive His Body and Blood oftener than hitherto, and wished them to seek Him more in the way of love than of fear. It had been wafted on its way across the Alps by the voice of the dear St. Francis of Sales, who translated its Italian accents into the tongue of France, and fitted it to find its way into the heart of that great kingdom. But on its passage northward, it found itself face to face with the stern spirit of Jansenism. It was not to be supposed that the religionists, who held in opposition to the Church that Jesus did not die for all mankind, could easily brook the less rigid discipline by which pardon was given to the sinner the instant that he gave morally sufficient signs of repentance, without waiting for the tardy process of years to assure the Church of his reformation. One of the chiefs of the Jansenist party wrote a book against frequent communion. It was one of their opinions that absolution was invalid if it were given before the penance imposed was performed, and in all cases they wished to revive the ancient canons, by which absolution was deferred until years of public penance had been undergone. It was not wonderful that men who had attacked the faith of the Church should despise her discipline too; but it was most lamentable that the spouses of Jesus should fall into the snare, and should not recognise at once that this want of sympathy with the mind of the Church of their own day, was an unerring proof that an heretical spirit was at work. It is true that no decree had emanated from the Holy See, making it an article of faith, that frequent communion was profitable, but there were proofs enough that the practice of the modern Church was in favor of it. If Marie Angélique had not been possessed with the spirit of heresy, she would have suspected herself of error rather than the Church of laxity. The Church is an ever-living body, and it argues a latent disease whenever the heart does not feel in union with her.

From the moment that Jansenism ruled it, devotion fled from Port Royal. The perpetual adoration of the Blessed Sacrament had been established there, and the first symptom of a change appeared when the Catholic world was startled with a new and extravagant form of devotion, composed by the sister of Marie Angélique, as a substitute for the ordinary method of visiting our Lord in the tabernacle, in use among the faithful. It was condemned by the Church, but still defended at Port Royal. It was not to be supposed that the love of Mary could long survive the loss of affection for her Son. Books were written against devotion to our Lady, as being sentimental and excessive. By means of the solitaries who retired thither from the world, the same destructive work was continued even after the nuns had removed to Paris. Port Royal became the central point of a great intellectual movement, by which France was inundated with works depreciating the traditions and the discipline of the Church. Under their influence all that was tender, loving, and beautiful in the Christian faith, perished in this fanatical attempt to bring back that which could never return. And as is always the case when men fall in love with an obsolete discipline, what they reproduced was not even the phantom, but the mere dead body of the past. They sighed for the ancient discipline which the Church found it necessary to establish at a time when men were crowding into it from a pagan world, and had to learn the very first principles of morality; and they forgot the daily communion in the Catacombs, of men and women pursuing their avocations in the midst of the bustle of heathen society. They did not take into account the Blessed Sacrament carried by Christians to their homes, as well as by solitaries into the desert, dwelling with them in their houses, and accompanying them on their travels by land and sea. In this zeal for primitive times, the Port Royalists did not even spare the Acts of the Martyrs. The beautiful stories of the virgin martyrs, St. Cecilia, and St. Agnes, were discredited, on the very grounds of their being supernatural, as though Christianity was not a supernatural religion, and as though there was any thing intrinsically improbable in the descent of angelic visitors or the outburst of heavenly visions in the dungeon of a martyr. They thought themselves happy if, with painful erudition, they discovered that the narrator of the triumphant death of a martyr made some blunder in the name of a Roman legion, or in the official title of some Roman magistrate, while they treated with contempt, even as a mere historical testimony, the fact that the tradition of the Church had consecrated the legend from time immemorial.

Such was Jansenism in its first stage, the most repulsive and the most dishonest of heresies. Its fatalist doctrines, its stern and arrogant spirit, its unmercifulness to sinning and perishing souls,—all is unchristian and unlovely about it. The attempt to remain in the Church when they were not of her, turned a number of men of great talents and great energy of character, into traitors to her. They simply attempted what was impracticable; they tried to be Catholic without being Roman; they attempted to believe in the infallibility of an abstract Church of the past or the future, while they rebelled against the present ever-living Church of God. All withered under their touch,—hagiology, ecclesiastical history, spiritual reading, and devotion. Their very pretensions to strictness of discipline broke down under the force of circumstances. They became all things to all men, not like St. Philip Neri, or St. Francis of Sales, but by a base truckling to the interests of their faction. They allowed of the impure romances of Mademoiselle de Scudéri, because the party was praised in the Clélie. While the Jansenist discipline was carried out in one of the parishes of Paris, and pentients excluded from Mass were beating their breasts outside the church, the Princess de Guémené was living in the environs of Port Royal. The severity of Jansenism could hardly be a greater guarantee for repentance than the mild discipline of the Church, when it was compatible with the impenitence of De Retz, and the feeble penance of such a recidive as Anne de Rohan.

As time went on, all these evil characteristics of Jansenism came out with greater prominence. The unerring logic of history has now fully worked out the problem, whether it be possible to remain in communion with the Church without conforming to her spirit. Antoine Arnauld died true to his heresy in the arms of Quesnel; Pascal went before him to the tomb. But if they could have risen from their graves, and seen the party which they served better than their God, in the days of its degradation, when ridiculous and indecent attempts at miracles, such as would disgrace a congregation of Jumpers, were performed at the tomb of the Abbé Paris, how would their proud foreheads have blushed for shame! What if they had looked forward some years farther, and had seen Jansenism in an unnatural alliance with infidelity, prompting Mirabeau in his speeches on ecclesiastical affairs,

THE SPIRIT OF JANSENISM. 19

pushing the prelates of France off their episcopal thrones, and investing themselves with whatever share of the spoils their new friends chose contemptuously to fling to them. Here was Jansenism in its true shape, a mere faction and a party; and like every thing which is a mere party, it hung itself on to every power, imperial or republican, which could give it a chance of success. Its professors were courtiers at Vienna, and wore the red cap of liberty in Paris. During the period immediately preceding the French Revolution, and during its first stages, the Jansenists were the tools of every party; their great principle, that it was possible to belong to the Church, and yet be her opponent in matters in which she was not infallible, and their claim at the same time to be judges of those matters, was a convenient weapon for a despot like Joseph II., as well as for the revolutionary leaders who established the constitutional church. The last miserable remnant of them perished on the scaffold; they were dragged to the guillotine by the hands of the men whom they had assisted to destroy the Church. Their betrayal of the Church had urged forward the assassins who shed the blood of martyrs at the Carmes, and they themselves in return became the victims of the evil spirits whom they had evoked, and whom they had not the power to allay.

It was during this second phase of the history of Jansenism, that the wonderful propagation of the devotion to the Sacred Heart took place. The lull of thirty-four years, during which the controversy had slept, and the Jansenists had remained silent, was broken in upon by a fierce tempest at the beginning of the eighteenth century. An act of feigned submission to the Holy See, accompanied by dishonesty, similar to that practised by Cranmer on the day of his consecration, had purchased for the Catholic world the interval of repose, commonly called the peace of the Church; and* a new act of audacity, no less shameless, threw Christendom into confusion again. But the controversy opened again under different auspices. The great combatants on the Jansenist side, Pascal and Arnauld, had gone to their account: on the Catholic side, Bossuet was soon to die. Port Royal was no more; after the death of the first Abbess, Angélique, the rule of the Abbey had devolved upon her neice, Angélique de St. Jean. Unlike her aunt, she had been tutored from her infancy in the principles of Jansenism. Brought up in the Abbey, in the midst of family affections, she had never had to go through the struggles with which her predecessor had renounced all that was dear to her for the sake of Christ. Her father, her sisters, and many of her brothers were at Port Royal; the graves of the dead were in the cloister, while the living were in the Abbey, or

---

* In 1702 the Cas de Conscience appeared.

in the solitude. She had not to renounce the world, for her world was in that valley, or in the walls of Port Royal at Paris.* She had all the qualities, good and bad, of the race; their literary powers, their strong family affections, their haughtiness and obstinacy. After Rome had spoken, after the episcopate of France had given in their adhesion, and even the poor pretext of Gallicanism was gone, under her auspices the inmates of the Abbey still held out. At length it was resolved to separate the most refractory nuns from the rest. Fourteen were taken away and placed in different convents. The scene of their departure is famous in the memoirs of the time. The tears which were shed were more like those of family grief, than those of nuns torn away from their convent. A figure, with white hair and majestic aspect,† confronted the Archbishop of Paris at the door of the church, as the veiled sisters were on their way to the carriages which were to convey them to their new abodes. It was Arnauld d'Andilly, who had come from Port Royal des Champs on a summons from his daughter, Angélique de St. Jean. "I had never thought to have lived seventy-six years to see this

---

* The original Abbey of Port Royal had been in a great measure transferred to Paris; there were two houses of that name, Port Royal des Champs, and Port Royal de Paris.
† Such is the description given in Jansenist memoirs.

day. I have there," he said, pointing to the Abbey, "a sister and three daughters;" and he asked leave to take them home to Pomponne, his country seat. This would not have been the way to reclaim them from their heresy, and his request was refused. But a moment before, when asked her name, by an official, Angélique, as she tells us herself, had proclaimed it aloud proudly, "for at such a time it was like confessing to the name of God, to confess to the name of Arnauld." She had fallen a victim to a fierce fanaticism; and it never seems to have struck her that the cause of God might not be identical with that of her family, nor that the Catholic Church, of which she stoutly professed herself a member, was more likely to be right than a convent of women. She was transferred to an easy captivity in the convent of the Annonciades. When released from her captivity, she left it touched by the indulgence of her kind jailers, but unbroken in her heresy. When the Jansenists, for a short period, made peace with the Church, by an act of submissive contrition, which we fear was wanting in the firm purpose of amendment, even then the Mère Angélique held out, and was with the utmost difficulty induced to follow the example of the rest of the party. She died in her obstinacy, and Port Royal des Champs hardly survived this its last Abbess of that haughty race, for the convent was dissolved, and the religious separated in 1709. The government of the party itself passed away to other hands.*

Quesnel succeeded Arnauld, with far less controversial talent, but with a greater power of insinuating his errors into the mass of men, and of reducing them to the level of the general intellect. On the other hand Fénélon was still alive, consecrating all his energies to the destruction of Jansenism. He effected in reality what Pascal pretended to do; without the adventitious aid of satire, he interested the world in the controversy, by exposing it before them in his own graceful and forcible style. He, too, died in 1175, with his dying breath entreating,

---

* Much has been made of the cruelty of this dispersion of the nuns. It should be remembered that every monastery is a corporation, subsisting solely by the authorization of the Church, and the Church could not but dissolve a society which, while it professed to be in communion with her, set her authority at defiance. A Catholic, at least, should obey the laws of the Catholic Church. Society itself could only gain by the destruction of the stronghold of a party, which taught a species of fatalism. It was the most merciful thing to separate them from contact with each other. There were but seventeen choir sisters and five lay-sisters, and several of them had the happiness of retracting before their death. Moreover, instead of being sent to prison, as has been supposed, they were sent to various monasteries, and their distribution was made by the Prioress herself. For the destruction of the building, and the disgraceful scenes that took place in the churchyard, the Church is in no way answerable. It is significant that Fénélon disapproved of it. Histoire de Fénélon, Bausset, iii. 363.

Louis XIV. to give him a successor who would carry on his fight against Jansenism. But after he was gone, the devotion to the Sacred Heart was doing the work of encouraging Christians, and filling their all but despairing breasts with confidence, notwithstanding the fearful progress of the now victorious heresy. After Louis XIV. was dead, the power of the parliament rose, and with them rose the party which all along had clung to them. The question almost ceased to be a doctrinal one; it assumed everywhere its legitimate form of a revolt against ecclesiastical authority. The Parliament of Paris had only been overawed by the authority of Louis into registering the bull Unigenitus as a law of the land, and now used that bull as a war-cry against the Church. During the Orleans regency and the reign of Louis XIV., the efforts of the episcopate of France were utterly paralyzed by the parliaments in all the measures which they adopted against the fearful torrent of infidelity and vice. Humanly speaking, it seemed as though Christianity itself was disappearing. In such a time as this, Christians needed devotion to the Sacred Heart of our Lord to animate and console them. It was not wonderful, then, that we find that devotion everywhere the object of the ridicule of the Jansenists. It was in Jansenist periodicals that the nickname of *Cordicoles* was attached to the members of the Confraternities. It is true that widely-spread as was the devotion, its work was too unobtrusive to call down upon it the direct attack of parliaments, but it is a significant fact that the prelates of France, who were most devout to the Sacred Heart, were at the same time marked out for the special hostility of the formidable parliaments on account of their courageous efforts against Jansenism. Four years after Louis XIV. was in his grave, the parliament of Paris ordered the letters of two bishops, in favor of the bull Unigenitus, to be burned by the hands of the public executioner; and of these two one was Languet, bishop of Soissons, the author of the famous life of the Venerable Mary Margaret Alacoque.

In 1720 events occurred which are commemorated to this day in one of the greatest cities in France, and bear witness to the triumph of the devotion to the Sacred Heart. Suddenly all France was alarmed by the report that the plague had broken out in Marseilles. The rich and the noble deserted the city, numbers of its very magistrates quitted the post of their duty. The parliament of Provence ordered the gates to be shut, and decreed the punishment of death on all that presumed to leave its walls. After this act of authority, the parliament itself fled before the pestilence, and removed to Aix. Before the fatal cordon was drawn around the city, its bishop, Henri de Belzunce, was entreated to follow the example of the civil authorities. "God forbid," was his answer, "that I should desert my people I owe my life to my sheep, since I am their pastor." During nearly two years, he was shut up within the plague-stricken city. For a long time there were a thousand deaths a day; unburied corpses strewed the pavement. The dearest natural affections were powerless before the fear of contagion, and almost all the sick, according to the Bishop's own account, were thrust out of their houses. Parents were expelled by their children, children by their parents. The dead and the dying lay together in the corners of the streets, and in the public squares. Amid these awful scenes, threading his way among the prostrate bodies of the plague-stricken, the Bishop passed every day like a ministering angel, carrying the Blessed Sacrament, and anointing the dying. His clergy nobly seconded him. Two hundred and fifty priests, regular and secular, fell victims to their love of God and man. The Bishop entered one day into a Franciscan convent, to implore the aid of the religious. The community was at dinner in the refectory, and the father guardian announced that whoever chose might respond to the call. All, down to the youngest novice, rose at once to offer themselves, and twenty-six afterwards became martyrs of charity. At length an inspiration from heaven came to the good Bishop, and he determined to consecrate his diocese and the town of Marseilles to the Sacred Heart of Jesus. The bells of the churches had been silent for four months, but on the fourth of November they summoned the faithful together. The Bishop, accompanied by the whole of his clergy, walked barefooted with a rope round his neck to an altar erected in the open air, where he said Mass, and read publicly the act of reparation to the Sacred Heart. From that moment, the number of the dead went on decreasing; till on Easter-day, of the following year, the people in their zeal burst open the doors of the churches, and insisted on Mass being said, so much had the fear of the contagion passed away. To this day, after so many revolutions, the consecration of the city is yearly renewed; and there is no doubt that the favor thus granted to Marseilles was a powerful cause of the spread of the devotion in France. Turn, on the other hand, to the history of the time, you will find Henri de Belzunce was a special mark for the enmity of the parliament of Provence, on account of his zeal against the Jansenists; and the temporalities of his see were more than once sequestered, in revenge for his efforts in favor of the reception of the bull Unigenitus. So true is it that a courageous defence of the faith against the Jansenist heresy almost always went hand in hand with devotion to the Sacred Heart.

But it was reserved for Jansenism, in a later development, and in a higher place to find out the full power of the devotion, and to attack it more directly.

After the doctrines of Jansenism had troubled the Church for a century and a half, the heresy broke out again in a different shape in the court of Vienna, and across the Alps, on the very frontiers of the States of the Church. In the hands of Joseph II. it had entirely dropped its doctrinal character, and its identity with French Jansenism would be utterly lost, unless we assume that the formality of Jansenism is a revolt against the discipline and the spirit of the modern Church, or a refusal to allow of an ever-living power in the Church to rule and command her children. If its doctrines about *sufficient* and *efficacious* grace have been forever laid to sleep, that peculiar shape of it which we are considering is far more common and dangerous. "The Church is infallible in doctrinal matters," was the language of Joseph II., "but there is a vast body of opinion in the Church which it is possible for men to disbelieve, and yet be very good Catholics. Let us keep to what is matter of faith; all the rest belongs to the jurisdiction of the state." And he proceeded accordingly to make war on all the discipline of the Church, and what concerns us most, on her devotions too. He abolished all confraternities, he laid a restriction on the number of masses, he forbade any devotions to be used except such as were strictly provided for in the rubrics of the Church. As Jansenism in France aimed a mortal blow at piety, by discouraging frequent communi so Joseph II. took it upon himself to destroy all the popular devotions which, without being indissolubly bound up with the Church, yet are tolerated and authorized by her. It was, however, in the Jansenist Synod of Pistoja that this spirit was embodied in rules, and took a definite shape. In spite of and in direct opposition to the Holy See, Ricci, the schismatical bishop of Pistoja, collected a synod of his clergy, the decrees of which have been severally condemned at Rome. It is in this famous Synod that almost all the practices of piety, universal among the faithful, are reprobated and forbidden, on the ground that they are not of faith. The members of the assembly lay down as a fundamental maxim, that "a great distinction is to be made between what is of faith and of the essence of religion, and what simply belongs to discipline;" and then they proceed to assume that the discipline of the Church may be most freely discussed, as though there was no competent authority to make it binding. They attack the administration of the sacrament of penance, and the giving of absolution before the performance of the penance enjoined. They condemn devotion to particular images, and the common doctrine of indulgences, novenas, and indulgenced prayers. They reprobate excess of devotion to our dear Lady, and finally, out of all the particular devotions of the Church, they single out that to the Sacred Heart as being novel, erroneous, and, at the very least, dangerous.

Jansenism went through one more phase before it perished forever. After the regent Orleans and Louis XV. came the French Revolution. One small party of the Jansenist body started back in affright from the rapid progress of this terrible phenomenon; but it is no want of charity to accuse the great bulk of the party of favoring it when one of their own body, with the Revolution in full operation before him, called the Jansenists its precursors. Forty Jansenists sat in the Assembly, and were the authors of the constitutional Church of France. Here again the Jansenist principle was patent, that the Church has no perpetual ruling power within her; they separated faith from discipline, and declared that they took primitive ages for their model when they introduced democratical principles into the Church, and caused the bishops to be elected by the people. The whole of the French episcopate, but five, refused to take the oath to observe this constitution, and were expelled from their sees. A very large number of the clergy followed their example, and throughout France the legitimate parish priests were expelled to give place to Jansenist intruders. It was at this time, amid the horrors of the French Revolution, that the devotion to the Sacred Heart was of inestimable value in keeping up the courage of Catholics.* One

---

* Berault de Bercastel. Historie de l'Eglise.

fact which we have been able to recover out of the bloody annals of the time, will be sufficient to prove it. It will show how religion was preserved in France during the reign of terror. While Carrier was deluging Nantes with blood, a gentleman, named De la Billière, with his wife and two unmarried daughters, were lying in the revolutionary prisons. He was accused of harboring a Catholic priest in his house, was condemned, and perished on the scaffold. His wife and daughters were dragged before the same tribunal, but not even malice and calumny could find a pretext against them. "The witnesses did not agree together." At last it was proved that they had distributed pictures of the Sacred Heart of Jesus among the peasantry on the estate around their father's château. They were immediately condemned, and shed their blood with the greatest joy for the love of Jesus.

Enough has now been said to trace the history of Jansenism, and to show its deep-rooted hatred against the devotion to the Sacred Heart. It has not been in vain that we have dragged to light a long-past error out of the obscurity to which time has consigned it. The ghost of a dead heresy may still haunt the earth, and in a Protestant country like ours there is always a temptation to be Jansenists so far as to pare down to the utmost the authority of the living Church, and to throw away from our religion all that is most offensive to those among whom we live. But the only safe way is to be Catholics in heart and soul.

It is dangerous not to follow the spirit of the Church of the time in which we live, since we may find ourselves unconsciously betrayed into the same cold and unamiable religion of the head rather than of the heart, which was the result of the heresy, of which we have been considering the history. Surely it should be a warning to all of us, when we see men of earnestness and energy, and of great austerity of life, falling into such errors in doctrine and such want of principle in practice, as we have witnessed in Arnauld and Pascal. And if it be said that few like them have either the talent or earnestness to be heresiarchs, Jansenism has its other phases too. Its subsequent history shows us how men may believe in the great doctrines of Catholicism, in transubstantiation, and in the abstract infallibility of the Church, yet may play into the hands of Protestants or infidels, by believing as little as possible, and rejecting all which, though not technically of faith, yet is the universal practice of good Catholics. They forget that what is commonly believed or practised among Catholics is an indication of the mind of the Church, since she tolerates or authorizes it. The devotions to the Church are the legitimate consequences of her doctrines, and a contempt for them shows that the doctrines have no hold on the mind that despises them. At length when some schism breaks out, or when the authority of the Church presses upon them, they fall away. The canons of the synod of Pistoja deserve study, because they are nothing but the rationalistic exposition of the faith and practice of a tepid Catholic.

Nor will it have been uninteresting even for those who are not Catholics to trace out the spirit and the fate of a party which has met with numerous admirers among all classes of men. The Jansenists had two qualifications for earning a great reputation; they had eminent literary talents, and they suffered for their opinions. But before we bow with reverence before greatness of intellect, we would wish to know in what cause it was employed. We feel no more veneration for the genius of Hobbes, engaged as it was on the side of fatalism, than for physical strength or any other gift of God employed in a bad cause; and the system of Jansenism has been not unaptly compared to that of the philosopher of Malmesbury. Again, before we canonize a man as a confessor, our first inquiry is, what were the doctrines for which he suffered? If he were to lay down his life in testimony of his unbelief in the freedom of the will, we would certainly refuse him the honors due to a martyr. The most astonishing part of the favorable judgment passed by Englishmen on the Jansenists is the easy forgiveness accorded by them to the dishonorable means by which they propagated their opinions. The only real and thorough Jesuitism, in the Protestant sense of the word, was Jansenism. It is conceivable that men should admire the courage of Luther, but even the world must excuse us, if we wonder how it spends its panegyrics on men who destroyed the church of France not by open warfare, but by remaining as traitors in her bosom. To prove this fact is like exposing an imposture. You cannot trust the autobiography of Jánsenism. Fontaine's memoirs may help us to get up a picturesque article in a review, but the result is no more like the veritable Jansenist, than is the meek Puritan of an evangelical novel an accurate portrait of one of Cromwell's fanatical soldiers. To learn the history of Port Royal you must sit at the council-table of the Fronde with De Retz and the Duchess de Longueville; you must penetrate into the secret chambers of the episcopal palace at Aleth, and hear Arnauld persuade the weak bishop to use a mental reservation, unheard of in the casuists of the Provinciales, and to disavow in a private document the submission which he was sending to the Holy See in the face of God and His Church. Finally, you must follow Jansenism to its closing scenes in the French Revolution, and see a Jansenist the comrade of Robespierre, holding a schismatical council in Paris, while the legitimate pastors of France were dying in the prisons of Rochefort or on the scaffold for the love of Christ. All honor be to the Society of Jesus, which from the first detected the spirit of this heresy and saw through its aims. Of the vast services which the children of St. Ignatius have rendered to the Church, not the least is the sagacity with which they discovered Jansenism, and the courage with which, through good and evil report, they pursued it; while at the same time they were ever distinguished for their tender devotion to the Sacred Heart of Jesus.

THE SPIRIT

OF THE

Devotion to the Sacred Heart.

CHAPTER I.

HISTORY OF THE DEVOTION TO THE SACRED HEART.

You may wonder why, at the outset of this dissertation on the Sacred Heart, instead of speaking about the wondrous love of Jesus, I should come before you with a mere historical disquisition upon the origin and progress of the devotion. And you will wonder more, when, as we advance, you find your thoughts broken in upon by the detail of events, profane as well as sacred. Our story will lead us from earth to heaven, and from heaven back again to earth: visions of saints will mingle strangely with worldly scenes; and the cabals of parliaments, and the overthrow of dynasties, will be found to have an unconscious influence over the spread of what had its feeble origin in the depths of a French monastery. I do not think, however, that we shall be guilty of any disloyalty to the most loving and lovely object in God's kingdom of grace, if we put off the consideration of it, as it is in itself. Believe me, it is not because it is interesting, that I would draw your attention to the historical part of the subject, but rather because it is the very best illustration of a great principle in God's dealings with His Church. It will seem like asserting a mere truism to you, to say that all devotions which arise in the Church are supernatural; yet, as we go on, you will find that it is true, in a sense which is not obvious, at first; nay, perhaps, when it comes to the point, that it is not so generally believed as the bare enunciation of it might lead you to suppose. One fact alone will serve to convince you, that what seems so simple, after all needs bringing home to the hearts of Catholics, and that is, that the spread of the devotion was not a uniform career of easy triumph; on the contrary, it experienced a deadly opposition, not only from heretics, but from respectable men within the Church of God. Now these good Christians, of course, felt no repulsion to the Heart of

Jesus itself; they would have been devils if they did; but what they opposed, with a strength indicating their inward repugnance, was the growing devotion to it. And this alone would suffice to show that there is more meaning in special devotions than appears at first. A few simple souls might have been left to indulge their fervor as they would, if in the spread of the devotion men had not seen a something which called for their worship too, a constraining power which, though they did not like to own it to themselves, looked like the supernatural, putting before them in their own despite, an object which they had not felt drawn to honor with any special veneration at all.

Now, I believe that the history of the devotion to the Sacred Heart brings out the principle in question more than that of any other; it bears on the very face of it marks of the supernatural; it does a certain work in the Church, for which it is especially fitted; it rains down heavenly influences on individual minds; and, what I would especially draw your attention to, it is meant by God to do so. All this will come out more clearly as we go on, and so without further preface, I enter upon the subject.

It is a common reproach addressed to the Church of God, that it is immutable: that, while all around it, arts and sciences, philosophy, literature, and all that adorns and ennobles this world of ours, are in a state of perpetual progress and improvement, it alone is unchanging, and what is more, unchangeable. Stagnation, a past and present without a future, one long, monotonous day without a morrow, in a word, all that looks like death, is connected in the minds of men with the Catholic Church. On the contrary, life, energy, and the power of producing endless combinations of multitudinous forms, are what the world especially claims for itself. It is in vain to answer that this unchangeableness is precisely what one would expect from a divinely-instituted body, that it is the very condition of a man's being a prophet that he should not change, since change is equivalent to self-contradiction; and how can any one, whose message varies, be the organ of heavenly Truth? The world grants all this, because it cannot help itself; but it goes on to say, "Keep your Truth, and we will keep our life; a Prophet, after all, must be alive as well as unchanging. If you are to be a living and energizing power, you must keep pace with the world, you must progress, and you must change. Movement is not enough: a machine moves, but it has no life; it does work, but it keeps on its dull, unvarying motion, and does not progress, because it does not change." Now, of course, there are many answers to the world's sophistry, deeper and wider than that which I am going to give. It is easy to answer that there is another condition of life besides the power of change; and that is identity: there must be sameness as well as progress to constitute a living being. Again, on the face of it, the Church does change, that is, possesses within itself the two opposite essentials of life,—personal identity, and yet that power of adaptation which enables it to meet the progress of the world. Look at the Church of the Catacombs; is it externally like that of St. Athanasius or St. Gregory the Seventh? Nay, look at the dogmas of the Church; of course they are unchangeable: God forbid that they should be any thing else: but examine the external forms in which they are presented to the world. Is the majestic structure of an Oration of St. Athanasius at all like the artistic fabric of a question of the Summa? No, the world has changed, and the defenders of the

Church have shifted their weapons too. St Thomas has taken for his organ that very philosophy, which St. Athanasius and St. Basil had despised, as the beggarly elements of the Pagan world. Here, then, is change enough to show that the Church is alive. But, short of all these answers, I am going to give you another, which will satisfy you, but will not satisfy the world, and it is this: the devotions of the Church vary with the wants of her children, while her dogmas remain unchanged. In order to show this, place, for instance, a man of the Middle Ages, a Cardinal of St. Gregory the Seventh, if you will, in the midst of modern Rome. Doubtless, it would be a hard task for him to recognise the material features of his ancient city, yet one, after all, less difficult than that of making out the meaning of other alterations which would present themselves before him. On the night that he quitted Rome with his sainted master, it was by the light of a conflagration, ruddier than the beams of the setting sun as it sinks behind the Sabine hills; and the retreating steps of the trembling fugitives were dogged by the war-cry of the Germans, who had won the Sacred City. But now the imperial arms, peacefully raised above the palace of the emperor's ambassador, would indicate to him that the relations between the Papacy and the powers of the world are entirely changed. If he inquired further, he would find that the foe to be dreaded by the Holy See, was not now the feudal Kaisar, but the Red Republican. Here is a change, indeed, in the outward policy of the chair of St. Peter. Now, place the same mediæval cardinal on the steps of St. Peter's on Corpus Christi day; he would find that the inward life of the Church had undergone some changes, as well as its external relations with the world. Let him follow with his eye the long procession as it pursues its way between the pillars of the colonnade; then let him be borne along by the crowd into the vast Basilica itself; the whole ceremonial would be no less strange to him than the high-raised dome and golden-fretted roof, which have replaced the gloomy vaults of old St. Peter's. He will recognise, indeed, the Blessed Sacrament, and fall down and adore, as the Vicar of Christ gives benediction to the kneeling crowd; but he will also see a rite which he had never seen before, and learn that the Church has, since his time, changed her discipline with respect to the Blessed Sacrament. He will find on further inquiry, that in the thirteenth century, an outburst of feeling broke out in Christendom toward our Blessed Lord under the sacramental veil; the life of the Church then manifested itself in a sudden gush of love, which overflowed the hearts of Christians, and a universal cry of joy from one end of the Church to the other, then proclaimed that the faithful had a deeper appreciation of what they knew well before, that Jesus himself, both God and Man, made each altar in the Church his home. In other words, a new devotion had sprung up in Christendom.

Now, this will lead us to a deeper knowledge of what is meant by a devotion in the Church of God. It is a realization of some one of the many objects which our faith places before us, one, therefore, perfectly well known from the beginning of Christianity to all Catholics, but not felt before by the generality as it should. In other words, it is a sudden love breaking out toward some Saint or Angel, or toward something connected with our Lord or His Blessed Mother, which had been believed before, but had not been by the world at large realized as an object of affection. From time to time it seems as if light from heaven falls upon some one beautiful part of God's creation of grace, and remains upon it, while the rest seems cast into the shade, and it alone appears to stand out to occupy the hearts of Christians, so vividly and strongly does the heavenly light bring it into sudden prominence. New means of honoring it are invented, confraternities are formed, and altars of precious marble and gleaming gold are raised on all sides for its worship; religious orders take it up, and theology is pressed into its service; while painting and sculpture vie with the sacred science in recommending it to the faithful. Sometimes the enthusiasm is partial, and confined to a kingdom or a city; sometimes it spreads through Christendom. As an instance of what I mean, take the Rosary and the Blessed Sacrament in the thirteenth century, or St. Joseph in the fifteenth, or the Immaculate Conception now, or, what is most to the purpose, the Sacred Heart in the seventeenth.

And now that we have got thus far, the question recurs—according to what law do these outbursts of feeling in the Church proceed? Is the light thus suddenly shed upon this object of Christian love light from heaven, or is it merely the offspring of devout imagination? Of course, if the question related to the dogmas of the Church, or the effect or reality of the Sacraments, it would soon be answered. But the matter is one, confessedly not of faith, but of feeling. The case is this: there exists in the Church a floating body of devotions, the use of which is not necessary to salvation, such as Rosaries, indulgenced prayers to honor certain objects, and the like; and to them again correspond certain feelings, as strong compassion for the afflicted souls in Purgatory, affectionate and tender love toward certain of the Saints, or certain mysteries of our Redemption, represented by symbols, which are also realities, as the Sacred Hearts of Jesus and Mary, the Five Wounds, or the Precious Blood of our Lord. And it is found, as a matter of history, that those devotions had their rise at certain epochs in the Church, or, at least, came forward, at certain times, with greater prominence than at others. The Church herself seizes upon and makes use of them as a part of the machinery by which she does her great work of saving souls. At the same time, she does not enforce the observance of them; and the question which I have started, is one which admits of discussion—in what sense are they supernatural? And I will just premise, before I enter upon it, that the question is an important one; for, I verily believe, that though the practice of such devotions be not necessary to salvation, yet that the way in which you are affected toward them is a very good index of your spiritual state. You may not be called upon to have a strong drawing toward some, far less toward all of them, but a repulsion toward any one of them is a proof that the tone of your mind is not in conformity with the mind of the Church. A great Saint, no less a one than St. Ignatius, has numbered among the marks of a Catholic mind, a devotion to certain objects, which we might be inclined to dismiss as contained in the wide class of non-essentials.* There is a profound wisdom in this dictum of the Saint, and I will now attempt to show you how deep a meaning there is in these devotions of the Church, and how certain it is that God meant them to do a work in the world, nay

---

* Among the criteria by which we may know whether we feel with the the orthodox Church or not, he numbers the following:—"The speaking reverently of relics, the veneration and the invocation of Saints; also stations, pilgrimages, indulgences, jubilees, the lighting of candles in churches, and other devotions of this class."

raised them Himself for that very purpose. Nor shall I forget all the while to illustrate the principle in question, by the history of that special devotion which occupies us to-day

I begin, then, by saying, even supposing I grant these devotions, and that to the Sacred Heart in particular, to be founded in nature, it does not follow that they are not supernatural also. Of course, the objects of Catholic worship are beautiful, and, like all lovely things, naturally attract love. But I would warn you against supposing that their action stops here; grace does not exclude nature; nay, God uses what is naturally attractive, in order to win us to Him—and when we think that we have been simply gazing on something beautiful, we suddenly find that God has caught us with his gentle craft, and that its beauty has been a channel of grace to our souls. For instance, it is a common thing to advise a poor soul, strongly tempted to a dreadful class of sins, to say three "Hail Marys," morning and evening, in honor of the purity of our Lady. I suppose that the sinner comes some time after to his confessor, and tells him: "Father, since you bade me say those Aves, I have not fallen into that miserable sin." Of course, the confessor knows perfectly well that the very idea of Mary, pure, beautiful, and holy beyond thought, as she is, has a natural power to teach us how glorious a thing is chastity. At the same time, he would be a fool if he did not see in that simple devotion something far beyond this obvious power. Taken by itself, it could only produce the wish to be chaste; but the three "Hail Marys" have, by God's grace, acted as a specific, and he sees, as he blesses God and our Lady, a supernatural power, exerted to produce an effect so entirely beyond its apparent cause. I, therefore, lose nothing by granting to you, what perhaps many might be disposed to deny, that it is very natural to feel love and adoration toward the Sacred Heart of Jesus.

And having got thus far, I go a step farther. You think it so natural to take the Heart of Jesus as the symbol of the burning love with which He redeemed mankind, that you are disposed to stop at nature, and to look for no other cause to account for the great devotion which sprung up in the Church in the seventeenth century. But if it be so very natural, why did it not spring up before? What is simply the product of nature appears at once, and does not wait for the slow influence of time to bring it out. Now, what is the fact? Had the Church of God forgotten that her Lord had a Heart, that she let sixteen hundred years pass before she suddenly bethought herself of it, and did Him the tardy honor of appointing a Mass and an Office for it? No, I cannot think so. She remembered it well, but it was not yet the time. There is a time for every thing which is not the mere offspring of chance. She kept her counsel to herself, and there was a meaning in her silence. And what makes it the more wonderful that this devotion had not come out prominently before, is the fact that it had struck great and influential Saints, many hundred years previous to the time when it occupied the attention of Christians in general. You would, perhaps, look for it in vain in the Fathers; it is too minute, too subjective, if you will, to suit the times of St. Basil and St. Gregory. And yet in an earlier age, at a time when, it may be, that the Devotion to the Sacred Humanity of Jesus lay more on the surface of Christianity, than when at a subsequent period the Arian denial of His Divinity fixed the eyes of Christians more upon His Godhead, there appears in the Acts of the Martyrs, something very like a beginning of devotion to the Sacred Heart. Certain it is that, in the suffering and deaths of those early confessors of the faith, a burning love for our dear Lord's Sacred Humanity comes out as the ruling principle of every thought and action of men, who could say in very deed, "I live, yet not I, but Christ liveth in me; and to me to live is Christ, and to die is gain." We need not therefore wonder that in the heat of the dreadful persecution, which broke out at Lyons, in the year 177, the image of Jesus should be most distinctly before the minds of Christians. Among its victims, foremost with the virgin Blandina stands the young deacon Sanctus; and when the writer of the letter from the Churches of Lyons and Vienne asks himself how the sufferer could bear the red-hot plates of iron, which burned his body into one vast wound, the only answer which he can find, is that "he was bedewed and strengthened by the spring of living water which flows from the Heart of Christ."* Such

---

* The translation is Neander's, in his Church History. The word translated "heart" is *νηδυς*.

is the witness of the early Church; now come down to the Middle Ages, you see it at once just where you would expect it, setting on fire the very heart of St. Bernard, and finding its way in floods of burning eloquence from his lips. But the remarkable thing is, that it never travelled beyond the gates of his monastery. Why was it not preached abroad in the ears of the world, till the whole continent, from the borders of the Seine to the valleys of the Rhine and the mountains of Switzerland, nay, to the very plains of Lombardy, with one mighty voice echoed on the devotion? The reason is that the Saint knew too well what he was about. It was not suited to the times; it was far too tender and too delicately beautiful to find an echo in the rough soldiers with whom St. Bernard had to deal. No, he preached another devotion, that to the Sepulchre of Jesus; and every king in Europe gathered his barons about him to lead them to the Holy Land. He founded the Order of Templars, and he gave them for a badge, not the Sacred Heart, but the Cross of our Lord. He knew that the material sufferings of Jesus would come home to them far more easily than the agony which wrung His soul. He preached the latter to his Cistercian brethren alone: it was not yet the time to preach it to the world.

Again, to trace the history farther, take each of the influential Orders of the Church as they arise, you find the same strong leaning toward the same devotion, without the slightest approach toward making it popular. It could not be otherwise. Look at that pale and emaciated figure, wandering among the rocks of Alvernia; there is a gentle lustre in his eye, which reveals to you the deep love of God which reigns within him; the wound of the side of Jesus has stamped its impress on his flesh, not less than those of the hands and of the feet. That heart could not forget the wounded Heart of Jesus. Accordingly, the first of his sons, who wrote books of devotion, the blessed St. Bonaventure, is full of burning thoughts about the Heart of Jesus. Yet even he failed in spreading the devotion; it never went beyond his order. Now, go to the other dominant order of the day, that of St. Dominic. I see before me a virgin form, and she, too, wears on her flesh, though secretly, the impress of the five wounds of her heavenly Spouse. O blessed Catharine of Sienna! the Lord came in a vision, and took her earthly heart away. "Then," says her historian, "all at once she was surrounded by a great light, and saw her Saviour bearing in His sacred hands a living heart, beaming with light. The saint fell down upon the ground, trembling, and with her face buried in her hands. Jesus came near her with a look full of love, opened her side, and placed the heart in her bosom, saying, 'Daughter, I have taken thine heart away, and I give thee mine, that thou mayest live by it forever.' Now, who so fit to spread the devotion to the Sacred Heart as St. Catherine? At one moment, it seemed as if our Lord all but gave her a commission to announce to men the love of His Heart. One day she asked our Saviour, in accents of love, why He had willed that His side should be opened after death, and He answered her, 'The chief end I had in view was to reveal to men the secret of my Heart, that they might understand that my love is greater still than the outward signs which I give of it, for while there is a term to my sufferings, I love them with a boundless love. Dearly beloved daughter! there is no comparison between the pain of the senses and the woes of the soul!'

It was not, then, because she was ignorant of its love, that St. Catherine says little in her works about the Heart of Jesus; nor was it for want of power of language that she did not preach it. The purest Italian welled spontaneously from her untutored lips when she harangued the magistrates of Florence, or astonished the cardinals with her untaught theology, or persuaded the hesitating Pontiff to quit the sunny Avignon for the malaria and the ruins of Rome. And yet none of her words, as far as met the eye or the ear of the world, announced her devotion to the Sacred Heart. Her letters bear on the face of them a love for the Precious Blood, much more than for the Heart of Jesus: she kept it locked up in her own bosom for converse with her Lord. Have we not a right to conclude from all this that it was not yet meant to be popular? Our Lord bided His time. Nay, there is on record a passage in the works of St. Gertrude, which at once proves the Saint's own devotion to the Sacred Heart, and contains an announcement that the propagation of that devotion was reserved to another time. We read in the life of St. Gertrude, that the Evangelist, St. John, once appeared to her, and that she asked him, how it came to pass, that, whereas he had rested on the bosom of Jesus at the Last Supper, he had written nothing for our instruction concerning the movements of His Heart. The Saint answered her in these memorable words: 'I was charged to publish to the nascent Church the words of the Uncreated Word of God the Father; but as for the sweetness of the emotions of that Sacred Heart, God has reserved it to Himself to make it known in the last times, in the decrepitude of the world, in order to rekindle the flame of its charity, which will have grown cold.'"* The doctrine implied in this passage needs no comment.

And now I have implied in all that has been said a principle which will throw further light upon this subject, and especially bring out what is meant by a devotion in the Church of God. I have been arguing that there is something supernatural in the outburst of devotion to the Sacred Heart, from the fact that it was withheld from the Middle Ages, and that no reason can be assigned for this circumstance in its his-

---

* The passage is thus quoted in Derouville's book on the Sacred Heart. In the Italian translation of the Life of St. Gertrude, by Lanspergius, it occurs, lib. iv. c. 4.

tory, except its being unfitted for those times. It seems several times on the point of bursting out, but it does not do so, for no other assignable cause than that God was reserving it for another period of the Church. I am now going on to show that there are peculiar reasons for supposing that God had a hand in its appearance at the time that it did at last come forth; and the first argument is one which will apply to all other devotions, though to none in the same degree as to this one. The very meaning of a devotion implies that it must be popular; it must influence masses of Christians in order to be a devotion at all. This is evident from what has been already said; no one would dream of pointing to St. Bernard or St. Catherine of Sienna as the author of the devotion to the Sacred Heart, and that, because though they felt it themselves to the full, they did not spread it or make it popular.

What, then, are the facts of the case? All at once, all over Christendom, simultaneously there arises a peculiar feeling of sensible affection toward a particular object in a manner never felt before. Of course the object is such as to attract love; but there are numberless other such objects in the Christian faith. How comes it, then, that that special Saint or Angel, or mystery, stands forth so prominently as at that moment, almost to absorb all devotion into itself? Why should it strike, not hundreds, but thousands, and tens of thousands of minds at once? I believe the answer to be, because it comes from the Holy Ghost. And in order to bring this out, I will go a little farther into the origin of particular devotions.

Generally there is an assignable cause for the spread of a devotion, and that more or less on the face of it supernatural. Sometimes it is caused by some peculiar circumstances of the day, and a sudden, mysterious attraction is felt in the minds of a whole nation toward some Saint, from whom it is natural to expect aid in particular difficulties. For instance, the other day, during the exile of our holy father, a strong devotion is said to have arisen in Italy to St. Catherine of Sienna. The blessed Saint had brought Gregory XI. from Avignon to Rome: why, now that she is in heaven, should she not bring back by her prayers the ninth Pius to the city of the Apostles? Or else some living Saint is the organ chosen by God for the spread of a devotion. For instance, it was the eloquence, the zeal, and the miracles of the great St. Dominic, which did the work of spreading the almost universal recitation of the Rosary. Or again, this sensible devotion may be the reward given by God to His people for their courage in resisting heresy; and I am induced to dwell the longer upon this head, because it gives me an opportunity of illustrating the dealings of the Holy Spirit with the Church, with regard to particular devotions. The great Catholic object of devotion next to the Blessed Sacrament is, of course, our dear Mother Mary. Now it would be absurd to maintain that there is the same amount of *devotion* to our Lady on the surface of ecclesiastical History, as there is in our own time; at least, in the technical sense in which we have been using the word devotion. In other words, though the faith of the Church on the subject could not vary, other objects seemed at first to call forth a greater share of the sensible affections of Christians. It is certain that this devotion existed in certain parts of the Church. St. Irenæus, so closely connected with the beloved disciple, brought it over to Lyons, and calls her in his works by the name of Patroness. Of Mary,

Tertullian has said that "by her faith she had destroyed the fault which Eve had committed by her credulity." While later on, St. Ambrose says, "Mary was alone, and wrought the world's salvation." Surely these expressions imply enthusiasm as well as belief in a dogma. Open St. Ephraim, you will imagine that you have made a mistake, and have lighted upon St. Bernard instead of an Oriental monk of the fifth century. All the glow of an Eastern imagination is called forth to sing the praises of the Queen of Heaven, and poetry is pressed into her service, just as eloquence became her handmaid on the lips of the sainted Abbot of Clairvaux. Still, as we have seen, the writings of the Saints alone do not suffice to prove the existence of, any more than to create, a popular devotion. While doctrine in the shape of a dogma issues from the high places of the Church, in the shape of devotion, on the contrary, it starts from below: it must influence the mass, before it is worthy of the name. Now, I believe that it is possible to trace out the time when Ecclesiastical History bears witness to a great popular devotion to our Blessed Lady. Place yourself in imagination in a vast city of the East, in the fifth century. Ephesus, the capital of Asia Minor, is all in commotion, for a council is to be held there, and bishops are flocking in from all parts of the world. There is anxiety painted on every face, so that you may easily see that the question is one of general interest. Most injudiciously have the heretics chosen to take the matter out of the terms of theology, and to ask, not only whether our Lord had a double personality, but whether Mary was the mother of God: more injudiciously still have they allowed the council to be held at Ephesus, the old see of Mary's child, the beloved disciple St. John. But perhaps they did not know the love of the people for her, of whose sojourn there, real or supposed, many a tradition lingered still; nay, perhaps the Ephesians were not conscious themselves how much they loved her. But now the fact is plain; ask the very children in the streets what is the matter; they will tell you that wicked men are coming to make out that their own Mother was not also the Mother of God. And so during a live-long day of June they crowd around the gates of the old cathedral-church of St. Mary, and watch with anxious faces each bishop as he goes in. Well might they be anxious, for it is well known that

Nestorius has won the court over to his side It was only the other day that he entered the town, with banners displayed and trumpets sounding, surrounded by the glittering files of the emperor's body guard, with Count Candidianus, their general, and his own partisan, at their head. Besides which, it is known for certain that at least eighty-four bishops are ready to vote with him; and who knows how many more? He is himself the Patriarch of Constantinople, the rival of Rome, the imperial city of the East; and then John of Antioch is hourly expected with his quota of votes, and he, the Patriarch of the See next in influence to that of Nestorius, is, if not a heretic, at least of that wretched party which, in Ecclesiastical disputes, ever hovers between the two camps of the devil and of God. The day wears on, and still nothing issues from the Church; it proves at least that there is a difference of opinion, and as the shades of evening close around them, the weary watchers grow more anxious still. At length the great gates of the basilica are thrown open, and oh! what a cry of joy bursts from the assembled crowd, as it is announced to them that Mary has been proclaimed to be, what every one with a

Catholic heart knew that she was before, the Mother of God! The Ephesians themselves were not conscious till then how intense was the love of Mary, which was buried deep in their heart of hearts. Men, women, and children, the noble and the low-born, the stately matron and the modest maiden, all crowd round the bishops with acclamations. They will not leave them; they accompany them to their homes with a long procession of lighted torches; they burn incense before them, after the Eastern fashion, to do them honor. There was but little sleep in Ephesus that night; for very joy they remained awake; the whole town was one blaze of light, for each window was illuminated. For many days after, the most celebrated prelates of Christendom preached on Mary's praises in her own cathedral, and the people especially flocked in to hear St. Cyril of Alexandria deliver in his majestic Greek a sermon, such as you might hear now in Rome on some high festal-day. Now here certainly is a conscious affection for the Blessed Virgin, energizing in the mass of men. A life-and-death struggle with heresy has brought it out. In other words, by the grace of God, here is a popular devotion to Mary springing up in the Church.

And now, let us turn to the Heart of Jesus, and ascertain how it was that a devotion to it first appeared in the Christian world. In all the other instances of special devotions which I have named, it has been argued that the fact of their sudden rise and instantaneous spread is a mark of their being supernatural and coming from God. I now go on to say that the inadequacy of a secondary cause to produce such a result also leads us to refer the origin of such movements in the Church to the working of the Holy Spirit. This argument is similar to that which is used with respect to Christianity itself. It is urged that twelve poor fishermen could not convert the world unless the religion they preached had come from God. In the same way, for instance, one monk could not single-handed have spread the devotion of the Rosary all over the world without the assistance of the Holy Spirit, even though that monk was St. Dominic. Let us now inquire into the circumstances under which the devotion to the Heart of Jesus took its rise, and see whether human means will sufficiently account for its rapid spread.

There is an element in mediæval Saints which every one recognises at once as romance, and which, without adequately explaining, at least points to one cause of their success. Look, for instance, at St. Catherine of Sienna, accompanying the young knight of Perugia to the scaffold, where he was to die for some supposed political crime. She had gone to him in his prison, and brought his soul back to Christ, had made him go to confession, and had been present at his first and last communion in his dungeon. Then as he was to die, she knelt like a guardian angel at his side, and whispered in his ear, "Go to the everlasting nuptials." With her own hands she stretched his neck down upon the block, and when the deadly blow fell, she received the bleeding head in her arms. At that moment, she says, "I saw the Man-God collecting this blood, all instinct with holy desires and warm with love. —What joy to see the goodness of God wait with love for this poor soul as it quitted the body, and mingle this criminal's blood with His own!" She looked unblanched upon this scene of cruelty, which would once have made her maiden's heart sink within her, because Christ had given her His own thirst for souls, and she came there to save one. "I, my father," she writes to her confessor, "have received a man's head in mine arms, and never did I feel a like thrill of joy. The smell of that blood filled me with sweetness; I could not wash it from my robe." It was because these red drops shed in a party quarrel reminded her of the blood of Christ.

It was her inauguration to a triple office which God had given her: she was to appear as an Angel of peace in the most savage of Italian civil wars, to cry shame upon the priests of the time for their carelessness about perishing souls, and to spread devotion to the Precious Blood. And truly the scene in her life which we have just described shows how well God has fitted her for her mission. But when our Lord chose to make a gift to His Church of the devotion to His Sacred Heart, he chose an instrument as little fitted as might be, humanly speaking, to do the work appointed for her. It might have seemed natural that the task of propagating the worship of the Sacred Heart should have been intrusted to St. Francis of Sales, whose own private devotion it seems to have been; but on the contrary, when the Saint aimed at influencing the mass of men, he did not form them into confraternities of the Sacred Heart, but of the Holy Cross. If the advocacy of this devotion had been committed to him, the all-persuasive sweetness of his eloquence would have been sufficient to account for the wonderful increase of it, without the necessity of ascribing it to supernatural means. But it was to the humblest of His daughters, that our Lord committed it. It is true, God has often, as we have seen, done great things by the hands of weak women in His Church; but in most cases, there is a high-souled enthusiasm within them, and a poetry thrown about them which fits them for the enterprise. But, in this case, it is far otherwise. Margaret Alacoque, a timid and affectionate French girl, had long been hesitating about quitting her family, and entering a convent. She had a vocation, and yet she held back. It was not that she feared the austerities of a monastery; hair-shirt and discipline were nothing to her, for her limbs had long been trained to the use of them. Nor was her world so very brilliant as to be a temptation sufficient to allure her from the cloister; it was only the world of a small provincial town. The loving heart could not tear itself away from her mother and her companions. At last she did make the sacrifice, and after a long and faithful struggle, threw herself into a convent of the order of the Visitation, founded by St. Francis de Sales. The rest of her story is soon told, for it has but few incidents. The convent was not a depraved, but it was a lax one; and she, with her strict and supernatural obedience, her thirst for perfection and her minute observance of the rule, found a heavy, ignoble cross in the daily insect-stings which the degenerate daughters of St. Francis inflicted upon her. At times, indeed, insult and outrage were heaped upon her, but in general she had to bear the slow and steady persecution of silent scorn. Her very confessors misunderstood and despised her; so that she found no consolation on earth, not even in those whom God ordinarily gives to fill up the place of father, mother, brethren, and sisters, who are abandoned for His sake. And what was more remarkable, the wounds thus inflicted upon her soul never seemed to heal, but ever remained open, bleeding afresh every time that the behaviour of the sisters forced upon her the feeling that she was not loved. She was, to the last, the same affectionate creature, keenly sensitive to unkindness, and expanding like a delicate flower, to every little act of love. No drop of gall ever entered her heart, for she ever loved best those who treated her worst, since she looked upon them as God's instruments in helping her to share the interior sufferings of Jesus. It was as if our Lord left her sensitiveness within her, stripping it of all that was sin, on purpose that her heart might suffer like His.

Now, it was to this gentle and holy nun that Jesus chose to intrust the spreading of the devotion to the Sacred Heart; and we will simply give the first of her visions, in the words of her biographer: "One day, when she was before the Blessed Sacrament, she was deeply penetrated with the feeling of the presence of God. At that moment, Jesus Christ shewed Himself to her under a sensible form, and caused the head of His servant to repose sweetly on His breast. It was at this precious moment that He, for the first time, discovered to her the inexplicable secrets of His divine Heart, and the treasures of love with which it was consumed for men. Then, filling the heart of His servant with a love, in some measure, proportioned to His own, He said: Behold my Heart, which is so inflamed with love for men, and for thee in particular, that being unable to contain within itself the flames of its charity, it is compelled to spread them by thy means. It wishes to manifest itself to men, that they may be enriched by those precious treasures, which I discover to thee, and which contain sanctifying graces capable to draw them from perdition. I have chosen thee, He added, as an abyss of unworthiness and ignorance, for the accomplishment of so great a design, in order that all may be done by me."*

And now that Sister Margaret Mary has her mission from the lips of our Lord Himself, now that He has made her the confidant of the sorrows and the sufferings of His Sacred Heart, how is she to set about fulfilling His bidding? He has laid a command upon her: what means has He given her for carrying it out? There were men enough in France, in the latter part of that seventeenth century, to help on the work of God. Bossuet was there, high

---

* The only comment which I make upon this is, to bid you remember how this vision is the counterpart of that of St. Gertrude, which I have already quoted.

in power with Louis XIV.; yet his commanding eloquence was not brought into operation to aid the poor nun of the Visitation. The lowly sister of an obscure convent in a little town of Burgundy, was too deeply hidden to meet the eye even of the far-sighted eagle of Meaux. Then there was Fénélon, the high-minded and unworldly prelate, still ruling over the archiepiscopal see of Cambray: it would have been well for him if he had but bent his bold and noble intellect, his fluent speech, and his perfect mastery over the artistic structure of his native tongue to the adornment of a theme well suited to his affectionate piety, and far other than the mystic dreams of the visionary who deceived him. And what was St. Sulpice about, that it ignored the lowly nun? M. Olier was dead, but his spirit still lived in his congregation, and it was the most influential body in the Church of France. If the advocacy of the devotion to the Sacred Heart had been simply intrusted to them, nothing would have been easier than to propagate it, granting that it was an earthly thing to be spread by earthly means. But God did not choose that any thing strong with the strength of earth should be the source of His work: He would have it all His own. In the case of the devotion to the Blessed Sacrament, which sprung up in the thirteenth century, an obscure nun, of no influential order, was intrusted by our Lord, in a vision, with the task of proclaiming His will; but He assisted her weakness, by connecting her with one who was afterward to fill the chair of St. Peter. But no such aid was given to the holy virgin to whom Jesus gave it in charge to announce to the world the yearnings of His Sacred Heart. There is no single great name of all that then adorned the Church of France, which is even mentioned in her history.

Poor Sister Margaret Mary! there is no more terrible cross in the spiritual life, than this meeting in one soul of weakness and of strength, when God forms in the heart a burning desire of doing something for his glory, yet leaves the creature in his native impotence. Jesus had laid upon her two contradictory commands; one, to proclaim to the world the devotion to his Sacred Heart, the other to obey her Superiors implicitly. Every attempt on her part to put it forward in the community was put down with a strong hand; and yet she was bidden to spread it abroad in

Christendom. She was ordered to proclaim the institution of a Feast in its honor, on the Friday in the Octave of Corpus Christi; yet, utterly unknown, as she was, what possible access had she to the Holy See, or even to the local authorities of her own diocese? Before she died, however, she had the consolation of seeing the devotion make its way in her own order, and even in her own convent, where at length a tardy justice was done her; and after her death it spread with unexampled swiftness throughout the world. If you ask me by what means the devotion became popular, I answer that I know not. I can only say, that in the course of thirty years, it numbered three hundred confraternities, in all parts of the known world, from France to China. I could be content to see nothing supernatural in a devotion rising in the hearts of a few devout souls. But when an obscure nun persuades the world to adopt a devotion dear to herself, when the movement originating with her, spreads like wildfire, and acts the part of a burning cross, handed on from country to country, across seas and mountains, from the Old World to the New, I can only see the finger of God, and believe that Jesus eked out with His Almighty power the weakness of the inadequate instrument which He Himself had chosen.

And now, one more argument to prove my point, and I have done. There was another difficulty in the way of the devotion to the Sacred Heart, which is not peculiar to it, but common to every other devotion in the Church. I speak of one coming from a quarter which you would not expect,—the Church herself. Let an outburst of feeling arise in any part of Christendom, the Holy See at once puts itself into a posture of jealousy toward it; if it be accompanied with alleged visions or miracles, so much the worse; the features of the vigilant guardian of the faith instantly wear a look of suspicion. The devotion spreads, and the whole world rings with its triumph; still there is cold, dead silence on the part of Rome. At last some of its zealous friends apply for an authorization; then all the official gravity of solemn tribunals is exercised upon the question; unenthusiastic theologians coldly weigh it; canonists plead for and against the evidence of its supernaturalness, with the acuteness and the dryness of lawyers; and judges sit upon it like a criminal. Let us not wish it were otherwise; this wariness of the Holy See is a drag, if you will, upon the devotion, but at the same time, it is its guarantee. I might have begun with this argument, as I end with it, if I had not wished to descend from the high ground which I might have taken, and treat the matter like one of common history. What is claimed by philosophers who are not Christians at all, for the history of the universe, is literally true of the wonderful story of the Church. Throughout the whole of the varied scenes which it presents, outwardly so like a mere episode in the world's history, so filled with intrigue, and weakness, and passion, there is God overruling the result. Nay, we may use the language of Pantheists, and say that the voice of the party, victorious in each struggle, is the voice of God, for we have that which is wanting to profane history, a standard to keep us from mistaking the workings of the human mind for the teaching of divine Truth. And that standard, is a very real one, as is proved from the fact that the Holy See by no means showed itself indiscriminately favorable to petitions in favor of the devotion to the Heart of Jesus, or to alleged visions concerning it. A nun in a distant portion of the world, as far off as the roots of Mount Lebanon, was said to have been favored with visions similar to those which appeared to the Venerable Margaret Mary.* The news spread westward from this lonely region of the far East, and the cause came before the Holy See. It condemned the visions judiciously, and mercilessly put down the confraternities which had begun to form in great numbers. After the devotion had been a long time in the world, a dethroned queen of England, who had lost her crown out of love for the Holy See, petitioned for a Mass to be said in honor of the Heart of Jesus. The demand was subjected to the cold analysis of the Promoter of the Faith, and rejected, not, of course, because such a Mass, which has since been granted, is unlawful, but because the petition was urged by its advocates on grounds which were dubiously tenable.† Afterward that very official of the Congregation of Rites, who, in his capacity of what is vulgarly called "devil's Advocate," had opposed the concession, when he mounted

---

* Berault-Bercastel, Historie de l'Eglise, vol. xi. 382.
† Benedict XIV. de Canoniz. lib. iv. 2, 31.

the Papal throne, under the title of Benedict XIV., himself, though indirectly, authorized the devotion.

I think I have now proved my point. To many I must have seemed all this while to have been taking a great deal of trouble to prove what every one knew and felt before. I can only say that I am glad of it; and yet, forgive me if I repeat that I am not so certain that you are right in thinking, in your simplicity, that it is impossible to have a repugnance to this devotion. Twice the Sacred Heart has made an inroad into England, and each time was a critical period for the Church of God. I believe it to be like a harbinger of storm without and of peace within; it is set up for the rising and fall of many in Israel, for a sign to be spoken against. The first time that it came, it seemed as if God was at last about to pardon England for all the crimes of the Reformation. The Duke of York, the heir to the British crown, had been converted to the Catholic faith, and, by his means, Catholic priests had access to the palace of Whitehall. The General of the Society of Jesus was asked to send to England one of his subjects, and his choice fell upon the Père de la Colombière to fill the post of confessor to the Duchess of York. It so happened that he was at the time, Margaret Mary's director, the only one who had ever understood her, and who had sympathized with her burning love for the Sacred Heart. Jesus had prophesied to her that every step which that devotion made would cost her an act of sacrifice; and now that there was a chance that the haughty spirit of England might be won by the love of Jesus, she was to pay the penalty of giving up her only earthly comfort. The loss of her director had won tears from St. Theresa, so Margaret Mary might mourn and be forgiven; she wept bitterly, and offered the tears which flowed from her bleeding heart to God. For two years the child of St. Ignatius went about this weary work in the crowded streets of London; during two Lents, he preached courses of sermons, in which the Sacred Heart was not forgotten. He made converts, and did a work besides, which he prized much more; amid the Catholics of England, ground down as they were by the petty, ignoble persecution of the Government, he found some souls with capabilities of going on to perfection, though they were wandering as sheep without a shepherd, having none to guide them. Just as he was beginning to lead them on, and they were beginning to love him as a father, there came a storm upon them, which put off for many a long year the permanent entrance into England of the devotion to the Sacred Heart The Titus Oates' plot broke out, and Father de la Colombière was first imprisoned and then banished by the British Parliament. He turned his back forever upon wretched England; and when the Duke of York came to the throne, under the title of James II., other men succeeded him in the care of the royal conscience. Yet, when through the errors of James, the crown of England had passed to another dynasty, the house of Stewart did not forget the Sacred Heart, and she whom we have noticed above, as the first petitioner for a Mass in its honor, was no other than Mary of Modena, England's exiled queen. The devotion probably still lay hid in England, and did secret work in quiet places and in humble souls. The next distinct trace of it, however, rises to the surface in the stormy times which preceded the Catholic Emancipation. The same parliament which had banished Father de la Colombière, was now inclined to cheer with its imperial smile the poor struggling Church in England. The danger, then, which threatened Catholics was, lest they should make a perilous compromise with a world which could not afford to be generous without exacting an equivalent. There was at that time a man, to whom, perhaps, it is owing that there should be a Catholic Church at all in England, who stood forward as the defender of the Church against Erastianism, at a time when many of those whom she had cherished and fed through years of persecution and neglect, were now inclined to barter her rights for the smiles of the world. We may hope that they are pardoned, since they knew not what they did. At the same time, we may safely draw the inference that there is an occult connection between devotion to the Sacred Heart and a hatred of Erastianism, since the first altar erected in its honor in England was that of a private chapel, where Dr. Milner used to say Mass at Old Oscott or Maryvale.

This is not, therefore, the first time that the devotion to the Sacred Heart has made its way into England. On its former arrival our ancestors proved themselves unworthy of what God offered them, no less a grace than to be the first land in which the love of the Heart of Jesus was preached. Oh! what a grace it was! It was an appropriate thing that the sons of St. Ignatius should bring it, as they had stood in the front of the battle, and had shed their blood for England. How St. Augustine, St. Gregory, and St. Mellitus, must have rejoiced from their thrones in heaven when this Apostolate of love began in England. The doctrines of the Catholic Church were preached, not, as in their day, under the broad oak-tree, in the bosom of the green forest, nor on the borders of a solitary river, but in the heart of London, in the halls of Westminster, and on the bustling banks of the Thames. Alas! we were not worthy of it, and it was driven back. The Church fell again with a mighty crash, and its enemies, with a shout of triumph, prophesied that it had fallen to rise no more. But it continued still its work of love, stealthily and silently, though it hardly dared to show its head. Many thought that it was so scorned and despised that it could excite no jealousy, and was safe from he dignity of being hated or feared. Yet, all at once, the mob of London rose upon it; a fanatic had but to speak the word, and red flames enveloped its poor chapels, covered as they were with the protecting names of foreign kings. The artisans of London, the inhabitants of courts and alleys, robed themselves in its spoils, and mimic processions with cross, and cope, and chasuble, danced with frantic yells around its burning altars. Yet, spite of all, its energetic old life remained, and it hardly knows itself now in its altered garb, as it stands up ready to fight, single-handed, against all comers,—taking up the double work which the Establishment contemplates only with an eye of stupid impotence, the Christianizing of large towns, and the defence of Christianity against the intellect of the day.

And now, do not think me fanciful, if I think the Sacred Heart is to have its share in this work. Have I not proved that worldly events have had a strange, unconscious effect upon its spread? Did it not come back into England at the very time when the powers of the world were forced to bring back into their councils the noblemen whom they had expelled, and the Catholic gentry whom they had scorned? Yes; and was it not promoted among us by the very man to whose exertions it was owing that this change was effected with comparative dignity, at all events, without serious compromise of principle? I cannot, therefore, be wrong in concluding that it is fitted for England, and that it is meant to do good there, from the very fact that it is now spreading. A confraternity was established at St. George's, the cathedral of the diocese of Southwark, some time ago; the sons of St. Ignatius set up another in its honor in their church of the Immaculate Conception. And now a third in St. Mary's, Moorfields, attests the unceasing increase of devotion to the Sacred Heart of our Lord.

CHAPTER II.

THE ADORATION OF THE SACRED HEART.

WE may have been surprised at the extent to which the devotion to the Sacred Heart has found antagonists in the world; and we, probably, have already drawn the conclusion, that it must be a great instrument for the glory of God, from the fact that heresy has waged such a deadly war against it. But it still requires to be accounted for, how it can have met with opposition among Catholics themselves. It cannot surely be supposed that the same motives which roused a French Jansenist against the Sacred Heart, can have found their way into the souls of so many Christians who secretly felt or openly displayed a repugnance to the devotion. And, indeed, I am perfectly willing to acquit many such Catholics of any so dreadful a disloyalty to God's holy truth; still, a deeper insight into the grounds on which the devotion rests will show that a great want of the keen instinct of a living faith lies, after all, at the root of the feeling, secret or avowed, which prevents a man from perceiving at once the propriety of honoring the Sacred Heart of Jesus. It so happens that we are now in the best possible position for apprehending this truth, for time has completely put us in possession of all the objections which can conceivably be made to it. It has happened to this devotion, as to many others, in the Church of God, as, for instance, to the Immaculate Conception. As soon as it was fairly put before Christendom, the undoubting instinct of the mass of Christians received it with a loud acclaim. Meanwhile, the opposition of those who had not faith enough to love it, found an organ in the intellectual difficulties raised by theologians, who did not at once see the whole bearing of the new practice upon the system of Catholic doctrine; so that now the whole question has been sifted to its minutest details, and we are in a condition to place it before the world, cleared of all the mists which were formerly raised about it. It is not, however, as a controversy that I am going to place it before you. It will conduce far more to the glory of God, and to the honor of the Sacred Heart, if I show you how the question raised by the obscure daughter of St. Francis of Sales enters into the very depths of Christian Theology. It requires only a love in kind, like hers, to love the Heart of Jesus; but it needs no less than a knowledge of the whole of the Sacred Humanity, as far as it is revealed, to be able to put into words why we adore it. Its controversial bearing will be plain enough from a mere statement of the questions involved. It will obtain a higher value in your eyes when you see that it is only a portion of a great battle which has been going on in the world around the Sacred Humanity of Jesus. From the time that St. John, the Evangelist, warned his little children against the first heresy, the spirit of Antichrist, in every shape and form, has seemed to flit from country to country, doing his best to corrupt our idea of Jesus, and to prevent His adoration. From the old brood of early heresies, which looked more like ghosts of ancient paganism than corruptions of Christianity, down to the more refined, intellectual, and subtle errors of later times, the way to bring them to an issue, and to force the demon within them out of his propriety, to show himself in his native rage, is to put before them the Sacred Manhood as an object to be adored. After the general principle has been settled beyond a doubt, the details are called in question; and the same evil spirit, which confused and troubled Christians about the Humanity as a whole, now raises a mist in our minds with respect to the worship of the Sacred Heart. Nay, the very name affixed to its worshippers, looks like an echo of the reproach made by Arians to the Catholics, as being, on their principles, guilty of the adoration of a Man.*

Knowing then, as we do already, from the decisions of the Church, that the Heart of Jesus is to be adored, I am not going to prove what your Christian instinct has told you already; I am only about to show you how this truth is involved in the very notion of His Sacred Humanity; and, in order to do so, I would enter with you, as far as I can, into the doctrine of the Incarnation itself. By-and-by, we shall have to contemplate the deep humiliation and sorrows of Jesus in His Passion, but just now we must fix our eyes upon

---

* Cordicolæ—α θρωπολα-ραι.

His glories and His greatness. It will be a joyful task for us to see how it is that every knee must bow before His Sacred Manhood, and how His Sacred Heart is worthy of all adoration, honor, and glory from every creature forever and ever.

And to avoid all ambiguity, in the very outset, I will lay down as a fact beyond doubt that the object of this devotion is the material Heart of Jesus, which beat in His bosom with a burning love for men, and which was pierced for us upon the Cross. It is, of course, perfectly true that one reason why we honor it is on account of the love of which it is the symbol; but let it never be forgotten that it is more than a mere symbol. The spirit, and the water, and the blood bear witness to the reality of its sufferings; besides being a sign, it was a very real instrument. Therefore, though, of course, it is taken as a symbol of the tenderness, compassion, and love of Jesus, it is not a mere figure and expression, but His own very Heart which we worship. Its pictured image on the altar is only in a relative sense the object of worship, though Jesus declared to Sister Margaret Mary that he took an especial pleasure in the honor paid to that Sacred symbol.

Still the Mass and the Feast were instituted to honor, not the picture, but His Sacred Heart which is now in heaven. Nor does it avail to say, that after all it is the Person of the Eternal Word which we intend to adore. Of course, the Person of the Eternal Word is the ultimate object of the honor which the Church intends to pay in the Institution of the Feast; yet we must remember that though all Festivals have this one common object, each has besides a motive, as it has been called, peculiar to itself.

An illustration of what is meant may be drawn from the art of painting. A painter may wish to paint a picture of our Lord. If he be a good Christian, the reason which impels him will be devotion to our blessed Saviour; and the direct and primary object which he portrays is Jesus Christ Himself. He may, however, represent Him under an endless variety of circumstances, as an Infant, or in His passion, or His Ascension; he may have in his mind various ideas or conceptions of our Lord, as being full of love, or majestic, or in sadness; and this conception, I believe, is called, by painters, the motive of the picture. In the same way, the Church, in all the feasts of our

Lord, intends to honor the Person of the Eternal Word as the primary object of adoration; but each Festival honors Him in a different mystery, or with a different idea, as suffering or triumphant, joyful or sad, or glorious, as the case may be. The benefits of God cannot be summed up in one single view; nor can one day gather up in its short course what Eternity will not suffice to honor. Each Festival-day, therefore, brings with it some new reason for loving the great end of our adoration. It is idle, therefore, to inquire whether the Charity of Jesus, or the material Heart, or the Person of Jesus, is the object of our devotion, as though one excluded the other. All these are expressed in different parts of the decrees emitted, and of the offices approved by the Holy See. When it is said that the Supreme Pontiff permitted the celebration of the Feast, "that the faithful might call to mind with a greater devotion, the Charity of Christ in His sufferings," the final cause of the institution of the Festival is put before us. But when the Church bids us sing, in that part of the office which most expresses her intention, Cor Jesu charitatis victimam venite adoremus, we cannot doubt that she proposes at once the Person of

Jesus, to be the primary or material object of our devotion, and the real Heart of flesh and blood, taken as a symbol of His love, to be its formal cause, or, to use plainer language, its motive.* We take it for granted, therefore, that the Church intends the Sacred Heart of Jesus to be adored, and we are only following out her intention, if we inquire now what degree of adoration is due to it. If in order to settle the question, we take a wider range, and inquire into the decisions of the Church with respect to the adoration of the Manhood of Jesus, we must bear the dry, logical discussion.

The question is a momentous one. It has been in every age the criterion and test of the heretical spirit. Let us then place before ourselves the Manhood of Jesus, and ask ourselves what is the adoration which we are bound to pay it. What we fix our eyes upon now is not the Godhead, but the Humanity of Jesus. We take the compound being, Man-God, and, without excluding the Godhead, we look upon the Manhood. Is Jesus, as Man, to be adored with the same worship as God Himself, or with

---

* This is taken from a little Tract by Muzzarelli,—Dissertazione intorno alle regole da osservarsi per parlare, &c.,—su la divozione al S. S. Cuore di Gesu Christo, p. 74.

a lower homage of His own?* We know that the Blessed Virgin has her place in the scale of beings above the Angels and the Saints, and that the very Seraphim in heaven bow down before her with a worship peculiar to herself. Now, in the ritual of heaven, has the Sacred Humanity also a worship of its own, above that due to Mary, but below the honor paid to God? Nor let us suppose that this is a mere question of external worship. Ceremonial is something limited, so that often, perforce, the same external honor is paid to a human being as that with which God Himself is worshipped. Incense is given to a Christian as well as to the Blessed Sacrament; and we bow the knee before a king as well as before God. But adoration is something deeper, and the question is, what is the feeling in our minds when we adore the Sacred Humanity? Or, to

---

* To use scholastic language, the question is: utrum Christus in quantum homo adoretur latria. In quantum homo is here used, not as though the manhood were *prescinded* from the Godhead or taken *reduplicative*. At the same time the Manhood, not the Godhead, is the thing on which the mind is fixed, when it inquires whether the worship of latria is to be paid to the object before it. Sensus est specificativus: utrum humanitas sit id quod adoratur latria, saltem ut res, quæ adoratur.— De Lugo. De Incar. Disp. 34, 2.

narrow the question as much as possible, when the Angels adored the Manhood of the infant Jesus while He was yet in Mary's womb, had they in their minds the same inward act as when, in the first moment of their being, they adored the Godhead of the Everlasting Word? And the answer which Catholic theology gives us, with one harmonious voice,* is, that the adoration which they paid to the Divine Infant was not an inferior act, but one and the same with that which they used to offer to the Eternal Word before His Incarnation.

Nor need we be surprised at this when once we consider what we believe about the Incarnation, and what is the very foundation of all our hopes. The moment that it is announced to us that God has become man, startling as the announcement may be, it prepares us at once for wonderful results. There cannot exist such a being as Man-God without a ritual of awe and adoration being thrown around Him. When once then we have ascertained who it is that has come down upon earth, who lies a sleeping child in His mother's arms, who

---

* Conclusio communis et certa est adorari etiam humanitatem Christi eadem prorsus latria qua Verbum divinum.—De Lugo, De Incar. Disp. 34, 2.

comes with dyed garments from Bosra, that "beautiful one in His robe," our natural impulse is at once to fall down and to adore. Adoration depends on knowledge, we worship that which we know; and we have only got to master the idea how it is that Jesus is God, and we shall feel at once how it is that Body, and Soul, and every portion of His Sacred Humanity, is to be adored as His very Godhead.

And, now, it is a bold thing which we are attempting to do. As long as we confine ourselves to the simple statements, which every child knows in its catechism, and say that Almighty God became a little babe, that He shed His blood for us upon the Cross, all we have to do is to love and to adore. But the moment that the understanding tries to grasp its own words, and to clear up its own ideas, how it breaks down beneath the task, like a feeble instrument, shivered by being applied to a work for which it was never meant! A union has taken place between two things, Godhead and Manhood. Who can adjust the terms of this wonderful alliance? When God called creatures into being, the Eternal Word sustained them that they might bear His own creating hand, lest, through the action of the Godhead, they should grow pale, and sicken, and die in the very first moment of their existence. But here we are told that God has taken up a Manhood into Himself: how can it endure this awful elevation? Must not He be degraded, or the Manhood annihilated? To stand in the Presence of the Everlasting Son is a task beyond Angelic nature, without the constant aid of grace; how will the poor flesh bear to be his own forever and ever? Look at the mysterious union of the body and the soul; does not the brain grow giddy with the ceaseless action of the over-working intellect, and is not the heart worn out at last by the wild affections of the will, to which it is unequally wedded? But here are two elements far more incompatible than spirit and matter. Will not the vehement rushing and the mighty flood of the attributes of God, utterly transform and penetrate the nature of the Man till it cease to be itself? Or rather, will not the fiery Godhead reduce to nothing the Manhood which it has made its own? And when the two come to act together as one being, how will the tardy intellect bear the awful energy of God? How can God rule the will without doing it violence?

Without the sustaining hand of God's holy Church, whose mind could stand the influence of these wondrous thoughts? Oh! unutterable faith of Mary, who pondered all these things in her heart, and looked them in the face and yet believed! Blessed art thou who hast believed! The rosy child, whose gentle breathing hardly met her ear, as He slept upon her lap, was the God whose voice broke upon the silence of eternity. And as he grew up before her, and kissed her cheek, and pronounced her name, how could she believe that it was God who looked so lovingly through those gentle eyes? And then his intellect seemed to gather strength like any other man's, and ideas seemed to flow in upon it apace, and yet it was the omniscient God who lay hid beneath it! Oh! blessed art thou who hast believed! And do thou help us to go forth and see this great thing which God has wrought, the Manhood lying unconsumed in the flames of the burning Godhead.

And now I must have recourse, like a child who cannot find words to express what it would say, to the Blessed Virgin, to answer the question which I have raised, as to the union of two natures in our Lord Jesus Christ. It is her old office to guard the faith, by stepping forward to defend the honor of her Son. The first heresy that ever rose, was answered by St. Irenæus, by saying that the flesh of Christ was not only in, but out of, the womb of Mary;* and it was said of old, that it was from her pure blood that His adorable Body was formed. And when it was attempted to be taught that Jesus was a separate Person from the Eternal Word, the only way to defend the doctrine was to commit the guardianship of it to Mary, and to proclaim that she was the Mother of God. I know therefore of no better way of showing you how the Flesh, which was formed out of the pure blood of her heart, is worthy of all adoration, than by drawing out before you how she deserved that most sublime of titles.

You will observe that those who first denied the hypostatic union, as it is called, durst not openly call the sacred truth in question. They allowed almost any thing; they said that the Godhead possessed, ruled, and dwelt in the Manhood of Jesus; nay, that it was the unction with which it was anointed. They exalted the Humanity to the very utmost; they

---

* S. Iren. Contra Hær. iii. 21, 22.

were eloquent on the wondrous graces bestowed on Christ, far above the Cherubim and the Seraphim; but they writhed like madmen at the very mention of the name of Mother of God, as applied to the Blessed Virgin. The faithful of Constantinople were often scandalized at hearing the denial of the term Deipara, from the lips of their Patriarch, in the very pulpit of the Cathedral. He pretended that he was zealous for the honor of Jesus; but he could not aim a blow at Mary without striking her Son; and if we place before ourselves what it was that took place in Mary's womb, we shall soon understand the importance of what they denied.

A miracle had taken place, such as never had been before, and never will be again. The Holy Spirit had come, and had framed within her, of her best heart's blood, a perfect body, and had joined it to a perfect soul, so that Mary was at once Virgin and Mother. Here was the nature of man all perfect: but if you look at that Sacred Humanity, in the first instant of its being, a wonder had happened to it, such as it has never entered into the heart of man to conceive. Before the heart had begun to beat, or the mind to think, before the will had time to frame one affection, the Everlasting Word had come and had made it all His own, and He who was in Mary's womb, was the God of heaven and earth. It was not that Mary's Son had been conceived, and then the Son of God had come and had joined this person to Himself. There was no human personality at all; the only Person that was there was the Everlasting Word Himself. He came, and He took upon Him all the conditions of that mode of being. When a mother bears a child, the body alone comes from her flesh; the soul, the noblest portion, comes from God, without any intervention of hers; but who would have the heart to say that she who bore him was only mother of his material frame? No, the whole compounded being, body and soul, is hers, because the person comes and binds it all together. In the same way God is Mary's son, because the Manhood, which was born of her, belonged to the Eternal Son,* in the same sense as each man's flesh and spirit are his own. And do not suppose that this was

---

* I need not add that the illustration must not be pushed into the Monophysite conclusion, that the Godhead and Manhood formed but one nature.

any superficial or temporary union. When once an individual nature has entered into possession of itself, by that mode of being called personality,* it keeps it to all eternity. God, by the very act of its creation, makes it a separate being, erects it into a person, and bids it stand alone forever and ever. It requires no new decree; God moulds a body, animates it with an intellectual soul, and at once the man is lord of himself, and enters upon a domain, of which nothing short of annihilation ever deprives him. Now, this inalienable right, which a human personality imparts, all devolved on the Second Person of the Holy Trinity. He had no rival in that Sacred Humanity, no one to expel, for no one had been there before Him. It had never existed without Him. Thus, the subsistence which it would have possessed, had it been suffered to stand alone, was supplied by that of the Everlasting Word. He gave it that by which, from all eternity, He had been a distinct Person from the Father and the Holy Ghost.

He entered on His new domain in the womb

---

* On the question of personality, see De Lugo. De Incar. xii. 3.

of Mary, the Eternal and Uncreated One; and, oh! with what a gush of wondrous love did the whole frame quiver, as in the first moment of its being, the Sacred Humanity became God's forever and ever. How the Everlasting Word loved this Manhood, through which He could adore the Father, and could pay Him a homage by the first beat of His Sacred Heart, such as through the long lapse of never-ending ages not all the Cherubim and Seraphim, nor all the Saints, no, nor all possible created beings could ever pay! He took that Humanity for His own, and entered into the most intricate recesses of its will, thought with its reason, lived with its affections, felt happy with its joys, and suffered with its woes. He offered it up to His Eternal Father, to suffer what He would; for He knew that it had given Him what He had not before, its own blood, which, by a union with Himself, gave Him the power of atoning for all the outrages by which His fellow-men had offended the Majesty of God. With what unutterable love He burned for sinners, and, seeing within Himself a very treasure of suffering, offered up His body to be torn, and His blood to flow, and His heart to mourn, if God would but show them mercy

Such were some of the thoughts of the Eternal Word with respect to the Sacred Humanity which He assumed; and it would be high time for me now to pass on to consider the homage which we owe to it. Yet I will linger a little longer on this part of the subject, because it is hardly enough to state the naked doctrine of the hypostatic union, unless we view it in its results. The mighty truth is utterly beyond us: we are all the while using expressions, which have a meaning indeed to us, because God infuses the ideas which correspond to them in our minds; but one which is too deep for words. The wonders of this blessed union can only be seen in its effects. Come, then, and let us see what the Incarnate God has done for the Manhood, which is His own. Let us look upon the majesty and the beauty which He imparts to it, that we may learn how worthy of all adoration is Jesus our King. And all that we are going to say belongs to Him as Man. It would be no news to say that the Godhead was perfect holiness; no, it is the dazzling purity of the Manhood on which we must now, if we can, fix our eyes. Of course, it kept its own nature; the Son of God did it no violence; it remained human as before, but on that Manhood was poured a grace, such as eternity will not suffice to comprehend.

That you may understand it, I would have you consider that every created being has one defect, and that is, that holiness is something accidental to it and separable from it. A plain proof of this is, that in some given circumstances it is capable of sin; nay, by its own weight it would, sooner or later, gravitate to sin, without the grace of God. But, as for the Manhood of Jesus, holiness is its native air, nay, a necessary portion of a state which is essentially its own. And this is why the bright sanctity of the very Seraphim grows pale before the resplendent purity of the Sacred Humanity. Theirs is but a faint and feeble image of the Sanctity of God; but in that Manhood is the very Holiness of the Everlasting Word. Some rays of the glory of God, have, by His infinite mercy, found their way to adorn the nature of those blessed Spirits; but the prodigal hand of God the Father has poured upon that human soul the very Whiteness of the Everlasting Light, to be its own forever.

Most wonderful was the beauty of that Sacred Manhood. One attribute of God belongs to it of right.* Immensity it cannot have, for it is but a created thing; His own omnipotence the Everlasting Word withheld, for He could not bring it with Him; but holiness He could not, and He would not leave behind. As it came into being, the unguent which anointed it in Mary's womb was the very Sanctity of God; and the fragrance penetrated and diffused itself through the very depths of His soul. Let God but create fire,† by its very nature it must burn; and thus the fiery flood of the Sanctity of the Eternal Word sank deep into the human soul, so that it glowed all over with that heavenly lustre. Light, if it comes at all, pours itself into transparent things, till not only their burnished surface, but their inmost being shines with its inward beauty. It does not destroy them, they remain what they were; but they live and move and have their being in the beautiful effulgence, which has made itself one with them, and has entered into them. In this

---

* Non potest etiam de potentia absoluta humanitas uniri substantialiter Verbo et non sanctificari; quia implicat contradictionem, uniri et non habere in se participatam naturam in que formaliter consistit conceptus sanctificationis substantialis.— De Lugo, De Incar. Disp. 16, Sect. i.

† V. Petavius de Incar. xi. 7, especially the quotations from St. Cyril of Alexandria.

way, at the moment of the Annunciation, the Everlasting Light of Light came noiselessly and silently, and poured Himself into the Human Soul at that instant created. No rushing sound proclaimed Him near; like a peaceful conqueror He made His way into the very depths of the human being, till will, and intellect, and human love, were all transfigured and could not move without the gleam of the heavenly splendour flashing in their every motion.*

Again, as light expels darkness, so the hypostatic union essentially destroys the possibility of sin. Up to this time, no being but might have sinned, if it had not been for the grace of God. The terrible evil spread like a cancer, until angel upon angel had caught the infection. The horrid possibility kept growing on into a dreadful fact. From choir to choir it flew, and each of them, down to the lowest rank of angels, paid its tribute to the miserable power, until the overwhelming pestilence spread down to earth, and perpetuated its never-tiring poison through the human race. One being alone there was who, from her closeness

---

* Petavius, De Incar. iv. 14.

to Him, was gifted with a sinlessness which was the shadow of His own; but what in Mary was a gift, in him was an undoubted right. Let her once be destined to be the Mother of God, there was an evident fitness in her spotless purity. But what was the result of congruity in Mary, was owed as a matter of justice to the Manhood of Jesus. Not out of God's absolute power could that Sacred Humanity have been allowed to sin.

Oh! infinite holiness of that body and soul! The Everlasting Word was bound to rule them well,* and could not let them sin without losing His own essential purity. Oh! ravishing beauty of the Manhood of Jesus! No wonder the kings of earth bow down before it, since the Father must needs love it, or cease to love His only-begotten Son; and the Son must love it, if He would love Himself; and the Holy Spirit fold it in the arms of His everlasting charity, since the very glory of the Word is on it. Come, let us adore it, since God wears it, not like a jewel on His brow, or a crown upon His head, but inseparably bound to Him as the con-

---

* This expresses the view of Suarez, De Incar. Disp. 33, Sect 2, on this difficult question.

dition of His human actions and the complement of His human being.*

Amid all the glories of the Sacred Humanity, you will tell me that I have forgotten the Sacred Heart of Jesus. But, in order to convince you that it is not so, we will now go on directly to the question, whether His flesh and blood partake of the wonderful effects of the hypostatic union. Recall then to your minds the symbol of this devotion, the burning Heart surmounted with a cross of suffering, and surrounded with the flames of ardent love. From them lift up your minds to its original in heaven, the material Heart of Jesus, and let us see now whether it, with the rest of the glorious Manhood, has a share in the glories which we have described. And I know of no better way of determining the question, than by inquiring what sort of homage is due to it, to see how far it shares in the adoration which all acknowledge is due to the Divine Person of the Eternal Word.

Here, then, is a problem to be solved; a new thing is seen upon earth, God Himself

---

* See the account of personality given by Petavius, De Incar., Lib. viii. 2.

joined to a human body by a union so intimate that it is become a portion of Himself. The very presence of such a being in the world must create around Him a solemn ritual of love and homage, such as had never been known before; and innumerable questions must arise as to the adjustment of the claims of His Manhood with the prerogatives of His Godhead. And in this, as in every thing else, the presence of Jesus has created an antagonism in the world. Against His Humanity, as well as against the Maternity of Mary, the efforts of heresy were simultaneously directed; and when it became evident that the Council of Ephesus would proclaim her to be the Mother of God, the miserable man, who had denied her the title, was heard to exclaim, in impotent rage, "As for me, I can never make up my mind to say that a child of two or three months is God, nor to adore an infant at its mother's breast." Two things, then, this subtle heresy never could abide; one was the Maternity of Mary, the other was the adoration of the Sacred Humanity. But it was long before it could be forced into the open avowal, which the victory of the truth wrung from it. Before that, like a serpent attempting by its writhings to elude its captor, Nestorius had done all he could to avoid the question. He had said that the Sacred Humanity might be adored with the Godhead, that is, like a separate being by its side, but by a different act. But the vision which the Church had fixed upon Jesus, the object of all her love, was far too keen and steady to be dazzled by such a subterfuge, and she proclaimed her anathema upon all who would not adore the Manhood with one and the same adoration as that which was paid to the Everlasting Word.*

From what has been already said, we can have no difficulty in understanding why this should be. It is a clear inference from the intimate union which exists between the Sacred Humanity and the Person of God the Son. If it be true that the actions of the Man are not only imputed to the Divine Word, but are really His, there is no difficulty in seeing how the adoration paid to the Son of Mary cannot

---

* Si quis duabus naturis adorari dicit Christum (in qua duæ adorationes introducuntur) sed non una adoratione Deum Verbum incarnatum cum propria ipsius carne adorat sicut ab initio Dei Ecclesiæ traditum est talis anathema sit. Such are the words of the fifth General Council, the 2d of Constantinople. Coll. 8, 9.

but be the same as that paid to the Son of God, since they are one and the same Person. But plain as this is, we must not suppose that the evil spirit which attempted to prevent the adoration of Jesus in the fifth century gave up the battle as lost after his first defeat. He has fought every inch of the ground, and has only given up each point after having raised endless questions, within or without the Church, upon the subject. It will be necessary, therefore, in order to place the subject in its clearest light, to go into the details of the adoration due to each part, as we have gone through the effects of the Incarnation on the Manhood as a whole. In this way we shall arrive at the Sacred Heart itself.

Place, then, before yourselves the Sacred Humanity of Jesus as it is in heaven now, or, if you will, as it was on Mary's lap, when the three kings came to worship it. Your Christian instinct tells you at once what to do; once believe that that is your God, you will ask no questions. You simply fall down and adore. If you do not do so, it is because you do not really believe Him to be God. If any one were to ask you the reason why you do so, you might answer: The Person who is before me is the Eternal Word, and since the Body which I see before me is His, I adore it with the same adoration which is due to Himself. And if you were farther pressed, you might go on to lay down a general principle, and say that whenever honor is paid to a person, not only its external sign, but also the inward worship, which directs and accompanies it, is addressed to him as a whole. There is no such thing as an analysis of parts in such an action. When a man bows down before his king, he does not separate in his mind the body from the soul of the being before him, and say, "I do not pay homage to that flesh and blood." He kneels before the whole person, the compound being, made up of body and soul, and to that he addresses his homage.

We may transfer this earthly conception to the adoration of Jesus. Christianity has only brought forward into prominence an idea, which existed before, though it had all but escaped the notice of the human intellect, that of personality. The Church uses it for her own purposes, and defines that there is but one Person, and that divine, in the Man Jesus Christ. She allows philosophers to dispute about what is the personal identity of "that thinking, intelligent being, which each man calls himself;" nay, she lets her own children hold any opinion on the subject, which does not make the whole question nugatory. But when a test is wanted to distinguish between heretics and those who hold the truth, she points to the Sacred Humanity, and bids all men adore it.

Let us suppose, furthermore, that a man, startled with the announcement that Jesus Christ, as Man, is to be adored with the same adoration as the Eternal Word, were to ask whether, in case he separated in his mind the Sacred Humanity from the Divine Person, he might not pay to it a lower homage than that due to God. The answer to such a man is simply what Catholic divines have given.* In a matter of adoration it is unlawful to make such an abstraction. Of course, supposing a separation did take place between the Man Jesus Christ and the Eternal Word, the Humanity thus left to itself would cease to be honorable, except as any other work of God, but adored it could not be. Strip your king

---

* Suarez, De Lugo, and Vasquez may be cited. The latter quotes two general councils to prove his position.

of his royalty, he becomes a private individual, and loses his homage. But, as long as he is a king, if you abstract in your mind the man from the monarch, and strike him, you are nevertheless guilty of high treason. Take a golden chalice from the service of the altar, it becomes simply a work of art, instead of being a sacred vessel; but as long as it is used for the sacrifice of the Precious Blood it is a sin to touch it, unless you have acquired the right by consecrating yourself to God, or have obtained a special dispensation from the Church. How much more is this true of the Sacred Humanity, which is not only the official representative of God, not only belongs to Him like a piece of property, but is His by a personal union which has been, since the first moment of its existence, is now, and will be, forever and ever. It is derogatory to the dignity of that Sacred Humanity, to have recourse to an abstraction, simply in order to treat it otherwise than it is. The proper answer to the question, then, is as follows: If by Jesus, as Man, you mean the Manhood separated in thought from the Divine Person, you are doing what is unlawful, when you separate or abstract it at all for the purposes of worship; for by so doing you mutilate the homage which is due to Him. If by that form of words you mean the Sacred Humanity, viewed as a Manhood, but still united to the Person, then it is to be adored by one and the same act of adoration with that paid to Him as God.*

Such is the teaching of the Church with respect to the worship of Jesus as a whole, body and soul together; but now another question occurs: What would be the worship due to the body of our Blessed Lord, supposing it were separated from His soul? Hitherto we have set before our thoughts the living Jesus, amid the joys of His rosy infancy, or, as He is now, triumphant in heaven. But now we must turn to His pale and ghastly body as it hung a dead weight upon the cross, or was laid in Mary's lap to be prepared for burial; and then ask ourselves what worship was due to that torn and blood-stained frame, when once the soul which animated it was away. We have only to ask His blessed mother to learn that she adored even those lifeless limbs with the same worship as she paid to the living Jesus, that is, to God Himself. As they

---

* De Lugo, De Incar., Disp. 35, 3.

wound the linen sheet around them, she adored His body with the same homage as when in the first joys of her maternity she worshipped her new-born child as God on the night of the Nativity. And the reason of this is obvious from what has been already said; the union between one of the race of man and his body does not cease with death, because it is personal. It still remains his, and will be reassumed as such at the day of judgment. Much more is it so with the Sacred Body which was formed out of Mary's blood by the Holy Ghost, and united to the Person of the Son of God. He did not put it on to be worn for a time and cast off like a garment, but to be His forever. Nay, when he assumed it at first, He did not disdain immediate contact with it. He would not permit the soul to interpose itself as a barrier between Himself and that earthly frame of flesh and blood, but He made the hypostatic union extend itself directly to each part of His Sacred Humanity. Thus it was that when His funeral was over, and the cold stone was rolled to the mouth of His sepulchre, even then the Godhead did not leave His body solitary. When it was left alone and none were there to weep over it amid the cypress trees of the garden, It still kept watch over it, and remained united to it as closely as ever.

One word more to apply it especially to the Sacred Heart, and we have done. Not only is it conceivable that soul and body should be separated, but the different parts of that Sacred Body may be divided from each other. And in point of fact various devotions to the Humanity of Jesus have for their object different portions of His adorable body, such as the Precious Blood, the Five Wounds, and so the parts pierced by them, and the Sacred Heart. Now there is one portion of the Body of our Lord to which the question especially applies, I mean the Precious Blood, since He poured it all out for the love of us. But I know of no question which can be more safely left to the instinct of a Christian. Who does not feel that his salvation is all owing to the Blood of Jesus? And if there be no personal union between our Blessed Lord and that healing stream, will it not lose all its power to wash our sins away? Be sure, then, that the hypostatic union did not stop short of that life-giving Blood.

Beside this, we may lay down as a certain

principle in theology, that as the Everlasting Word united to Himself a perfect human nature, so in rising again He left out nothing which was necessary to its reality. Further, it is believed that the hypostatic union never deserted whatever, being a real part of the bodily frame, was ultimately ever to remain within it. No drop, therefore, of the Precious Blood, which was united to Him at the resurrection, ever lost this union. How anxiously, then, did angels keep watch and ward over those red drops wherever they lay, during the three days when He lay in the tomb. He had shed it everywhere for us like a very deluge; and everywhere during that fearful day and night His steps might have been tracked by blood. It began to roll from His pallid brow in crimson beads, till His garments were stained, and the green grass beneath the olive-trees was bedewed with the precious drops. The scourge drank deep into it, and the ponits of His thorny crown were clotted over with its dark red stains. It lay upon the broad highway, and beneath the cross itself. But wherever it was found, there were angels adoring, because they saw His Divine Person still united to it, and they knew well that on the third day it would be restored to the Sacred Heart from whence it came.

If, then, it had been true that during those three days, the Sacred Heart had been really separated from the rest of the adorable Humanity, it would nevertheless be itself an object of adoration, because that separation would not have caused it to be deserted by the Person of the Everlasting Word. At the same time such a supposition is not necessary to our purpose. The object of our devotion is the living Heart, as it is in heaven now glorified with the rest of the Humanity of our blessed Lord. In order to establish this more clearly, we have only to point to a passage in the bull which condemned the Synod of Pistoja. The pretended council is condemned "because it blames the worshippers of the Heart of Jesus for not observing that neither the most holy flesh of Christ, nor any part of it, nor even the whole Manhood, separated or abstracted from the Godhead, is to be adored with the worship of latria." "As though," the bull continues, "the faithful did adore the Heart of Jesus, separated or abstracted from the Godhead, when they adore it as the Heart of Jesus, the Heart of the Person of the Word, to whom it is inseparably united. In the same way the bloodless body of Jesus Christ during the three days of death is adorable in the tomb, being neither separated nor abstracted from the Godhead."

At length, then, we have reached the term which we proposed to ourselves at the beginning of this inquiry. If it has been long and weary, it will at least have served to show how profoundly rooted in the Christian faith are devotions to the Sacred Humanity of Jesus. They are not dead things, lying like fossils, imbedded in the remains of a world gone by; but the entire system is living, so that you cannot touch the smallest part without affecting the whole. We can see now why it is that the power of the devil has ever been directed with such unexampled pertinacity against these simple devotions to the adorable Manhood. It is simply because they bear witness to the adoration of Jesus as Man.

No wonder, then, that these lost spirits stir up all the powers of hell against them. They remember in their terrible despair that the very cause of their being hurled from heaven was their refusal to bow down before the decree of God, which announced that all, even angelic spirits, would have to adore the Incarnate Word. No wonder that they wage war against the idea of personality in every shape that it comes before them. They see well how it involves the eternal responsibility of a human being. In heathen times they so obscured it that it was well-nigh forgotten. They still cloud over every doctrine which reminds men of the personality of each individual human being, such as the eternity of divine punishment, and the resurrection of the body. The reality of this idea is brought into clear and unmistakable prominence by the Incarnation of the Word, and they try to destroy that doctrine by ceaseless efforts. They have even attempted to rival and to imitate the Incarnation. This is why devils enter into men by possession. They thus do their best to make a human body and soul their own, so as seemingly to destroy the personality of that being, and to assume it themselves; though of course this turns to their own degradation, through the all-powerful name of Jesus, and the exorcisms of the Church. But their greatest aim is to inspire the intellect of man to invent new heresies, which deny this mighty truth, or prevent men from adoring the Sacred Humanity.

The last of these efforts is the war directed against the devotion to the Sacred Heart. It is no isolated phenomenon. It is only one act in that great battle against the adoration of Jesus as Man, which began with the fall of the angels, and will end only with the day of judgment. Its connection with heresy is no longer occult to us. We can no longer wonder that doctrinal error or Erastianism, that heresy of worldliness, so often accompanies repugnance to devotions to the Sacred Heart. Disobedience to the Holy See, opposition to Catholic devotions, low conceptions of Mary's honor, all seem to form a sort of organic whole. It is not that they have any thing substantial in themselves; it is that all are symptoms of the heretical spirit, which, like a disease, lurks about the souls of all who are not thoroughly loyal children of the Church, ready to throw itself out at any moment and in any shape. By the grace of God the enemy of mankind never will succeed in destroying the simplicity and the child-like devotions of Catholics. They will follow the instincts of their hearts, and only cry out forever—

Praise, blessing, love, service, and glory, be everywhere, and forever, to the divine Heart of Jesus, and the Immaculate Heart of Mary! Amen.

CHAPTER III.

THE LOVE OF THE HEART OF JESUS.

An infidel philosopher has laid down the astonishing sentiment, that "He who loves God aright must not require that God should love him in return." But this is not the feeling of a Christian, nor even the language of the natural human heart. To the honor of mankind, fallen as we are, there has ever remained in the recesses of our being a powerful attraction toward God, a remnant of our original justice. As a nation, expelled from its first home, preserves a faint tradition of the country which it has left, so it seems as though the race of man keeps still a melancholy remembrance of its old supernatural state, and still longs to love God and be loved by Him. The very errors about the nature of God, into which men have fallen, show the tenacity with which they cling to the idea of His existence. It is as though they felt a longing desire to know how He would receive them if they sought His face again. They looked into their own hearts, and found a living energy utterly wasted; a power of loving without an end or an object, unless there was a God whom they could love. Such was the language of their hearts, the cry of their inward consciousness. On the other hand, who or what was there to give them news about the character of their God? The external world cried out that there was a God, but could it tell them how He regarded them, or how they might regard Him? Did He love them, or did He hate them? Might they dare to love Him?

If they looked abroad on Nature, she could not solve the mystery. There was a very music of peace and calm in the majesty of the stars and the holy beauty of the flowers; but all this was nature unfallen, and was not there enough besides to point to some convulsion, some subsequent rupture between the Creator and His creatures? Was not the face of the earth seamed and scarred all over with the marks of His wrath, and did not the volcano and the pestilence tell a different tale from the corn, and wine, and oil, which God gives to make glad the heart of man? Hence, men in absolute despair rushed into the most opposite opinions about God, and side by side with each other were cruel and bloody rites, and religions breathing the very spirit of voluptuousness. With some, God was a good-natured being, who wished His creatures to enjoy themselves, as far as He cared about them at all; in whom the permission of suffering was the effect of carelessness, and to whose nature the infliction of pain as a punishment was utterly foreign. On the other hand were ranged the stern old religions, which propitiated God with human victims, and gave the fruit of the body for the sin of the soul. They looked upon God as an almighty demon, with unbounded powers and inexorable will.

Miserable state of mankind! to feel powerfully drawn to God, and yet not to dare to approach Him! What could prevent them from rushing into the arms of their God, since they were ever open to receive those who sought Him? The only reason why they hung back was, that they did not know how loving and how good He is. They had lost the belief that He would bestow the rich guerdon of His love

on all who diligently seek Him. Without this
the soul was unable to elicit from its depths an
act of the sovereign love of God.* In vain did
the foulness of sin come upon them by a miserable
experience; it did not drive them to
Him. Attribute after attribute of God seemed
to woo them to Him: but they did not solve
the question, could we love Him, and would He
love us in return? Beauty, majesty, and purity,
produce cold admiration, and affect not
the heart, till the being who possesses them
proves his title to love by showing that he is
loving. Nature might reveal the wonders of
God; it was a display of wonderful power, and
proved the subtle influence of some viewless
almighty spirit, but it told too little of the personal
moral character of its Creator, to bid us
firmly hope for a mutual love. Such is the nature
of the heart of man, it will not bestow its
love except when it can hope for a requital.
It cannot love by the word of command, for
love must flow from the spontaneous spring of
the unbought heart. Show me that thou canst

---

* See De Lugo, De Virt. Fid. Div. Disp. 12, 5, on the question
why the natural powers, without faith, are insufficient to
produce an act of the sovereign love of God.

love if thou wouldst have me love,* is the language which it holds even to its God. But was it in his nature to love? Can he feel for His poor creatures without feeling, compassionate them without suffering, love them and yet be passionless?

Such is the language which the human heart would use; the old tradition of the God who spoke of old to Adam in accents of love amid the trees of Paradise, was more and more obscured. Faith in God as a loving being had disappeared from earth; hope and love had perished with it; and when every motive which stirs the heart of man, had ceased to lift him to heaven, what would he do but turn the whole of his mighty powers of loving to earth? What but the faith in a loving God has enough of heaven in it to keep the soul from the visible joys of sin? As for the beauty of virtue and the ugliness of vice, they may sway the young hearts of men and of nations for a time, but they are soon swept out of the way by the mighty deluge of corruption and the fierce tempest of wild passion. Nay, after the trembling soul has lost its balance, and has committed its

---

* Vis ut ameris, ama. De Lugo, ubi. sup.

first sin, the sense of guilt comes upon it more deeply in proportion to its love of virtue, and frightens it away from God. Then, over and above what was there before, comes upon the soul a new and terrible doubt—will God forgive? The Indian penance and the prevalence of human sacrifices bear sufficient witness to the power of this terrible doubt. Reason might or might not conclude in favor of mercy; but its highest effort could not do away with doubt in the face of the awful silence of God himself. That he did punish was certain; earth bore sufficient signs that his justice was provided for in its very structure, and interwoven with the very laws of the race that dwelt on its surface. Was there any proof that he ever forgave?

Such is the state of man not under the dominion of grace; enough of God is left to seek Him, but not enough to find Him; enough to fear Him, yet not enough to love Him above all things. While he clings desperately to the thought of the existence of his God, he is ever impatient of the presence of a being whose character is so uncertain, while His power is so palpable. The very love of the heart of man was so turned to selfishness, that it was often a greater curse than his hatred, since it corrupted both himself and the object of his affection. His very God was without any moral nature at all, and had degenerated into the mere principle of life, worshipped in plant, or in tree, or animal. Or else there was a God of simple destruction side by side with a God of simple love, sharing thus a divided empire, or waging a doubtful contest with his rival. And further on in the far East was the god of transmigration, impersonal himself, and the destruction of personality in all others, since the fatal union with him reduced the individual to nothingness in his embrace. Or to complete the circle of the globe, take that vast portion of the race of man which had been forgotten across the Atlantic, and had dropped off from their fellows, and so had become the purest representatives of mere nature, without any admixture of divine tradition. Their gods are to be sought for in the spirits which animated the bodies of wild animals. The highest conception of the divine character to which they attained was embodied in the cunning and ferocity of the instinct of brutes; while in the empires created by their spontaneous civilization, human sacrifices bore witness to their notion of the cruelty of God.

Such is the product of the efforts of the mass of mankind in their unassisted search after the God that they had lost; such the striking witness borne by history to the conclusion of a great theologian, that no notion of God save that of the loving being whom faith reveals to us, ever elicited from the heart of man an act of the love of God above all things. So impossible is it for man to keep, without faith, the true conception of God; He degrades His mercy into simple absolute benevolence, or he forgets it altogether. He imagines and worships, as men do now, a being of effeminate clemency and finite justice, with a universal heaven, and a temporary hell; or else he creates for himself a God of simple vengeance, and shrinks back from his own creation. Both these views, however opposite, have thus much in common, that they render the love of God above all things impossible, even as a transient act. Neither of these is our loving God, who loves the sinner in spite of His hatred of sin, who is merciful, though He is just.

Who is there that can bestow confidence between man and his Creator? Who is there that will tell mankind how loving is God, although He is purity itself? The voice of

God Himself alone can reassure His creatures; and all at once he speaks. A message comes from heaven, and this time it is not brought by an ambassador; it is God Himself who brings it. It is the voice of the Eternal Father, speaking through His Son; God has so loved the world, that He gave His only-begotten Son. It is the voice of the everlasting Word: A body hast Thou prepared for me. Lo! I am come to do Thy will, O God. Behold, I am on earth to do Thy will, and Thy will is to tell men how loving Thou art; and it is for this I have come with the love of a God burning within me; I bear it in my bosom, enshrined and concentred in a human Heart. And the Holy Spirit too must have His share in the work; He drew the Heart of Jesus from the blood of a Virgin Mother. He framed it with a view to suffering, and placed within it the infinite capacity of loving, and the boundless power of suffering which belong to a human soul.

Such, then, is the spirit of devotion to the Sacred Heart; its end and object is not only adoration, but love. Mankind have doubted whether God could love; they could not understand love without passion and without feeling. To solve the tormenting doubt, God came down from heaven with a human heart brimful of love, throbbing and palpitating with every human emotion, yet without sin. It is this very Heart of flesh and blood which we adore in this devotion; but besides this worship, we take it as a symbol of love. Just as when we say of our friend that his heart is full of love, we take his real heart as a type of his affections; so Jesus, condescending to our language, speaks of His own Heart as full of love.* The heart of man is like a sacrament; it is both the sign and the organ of love; and when men in their ingratitude forget how loving He is, He points to His Sacred Heart, and bids His servants spread devotion to it far and wide, as an outward and visible sign of the love which He bears them.

Here, then, we have arrived at the spirit of the devotion to the Sacred Heart; it is the worship of the love of Jesus. The devotion to the Five Wounds, or to the Precious Blood, or to the Holy Cross, are all equally addressed to the Person of Jesus, but they all differ from that which occupies us now in the spirit which animates them. While they all apply espe-

---

* Life of Ven. Margaret Mary Alacoque, vol. i. p. 187.

cially to the Passion in its different phases of suffering, intercessory power, and triumph, this one has a peculiar and direct reference to the love of Jesus throughout His life. The collect in the Missal points not only to the Passion, but in general to the "benefits which are the result of the love of the Heart of Jesus." "Cor Jesu charitate vulneratum venite adoremus," is the invitatory of the office in the Breviary; and in the brief which authorizes the devotion, its end and object is stated to be "to promote the memory of the love of the Lord."

It is as though in this devotion God entered into a controversy with His people and challenged them to show Him what He could have done more to prove to them how He loved them. They feel that the Godhead is so high above them that they doubt of its power of loving, on the ground that it cannot feel pity and compassion. Here, then, to do away with their fears, is God loving with a human heart. Let them examine and see whether they can find another heart more loving and compassionate than His. Here is the character of God expressed in human terms, and level with human understanding. The human Heart of

Jesus has given us the power of measuring the love of God, of comprehending the incomprehensible. We will therefore use the power which it gives us, and by taking it as the standard of the love of God, we will show the injustice of man in doubting of His lovingness. And in order to do so, we will analyze the love of the Sacred Heart of Jesus. We will see what influence the Godhead has over it. Does it augment or take away from its power of loving? We will take God's side in the matter, and answer the doubts which make men tremblingly inquire whether God can really be loving or not. Can there be love in God, since love is a passion? is the secret language of the human soul. Can there be mercy, since He cannot feel?* We know that there is love in the Godhead. We have heard of old that the Father loves the Son; and the Holy Spirit is the eternal fruit of the gaze of love which the Father has fixed forever on the beautiful face of His everlasting Word. And the Son loves the Father, for the same Spirit proceeds from them both as from one fountain of Love, and

---

* Videtur quod amor non sit in Deo; nulla enim passio est in Deo, Summa, i. 20, is the objection which St. Thomas puts to himself.

is Himself the very uncreated joy of their mutual indwelling. But can the infinite stoop to love the finite? Can God love us? God's answer to the cry of mankind is the Heart of Jesus.

Let no one, therefore, think that in speaking of the love of Jesus, we would deny that as God He is loving. On the contrary, our very object is to show how, because He is God, the whole Frame of Jesus, in His Sacred Humanity, thrills with love, how His heart is raised to a power of loving beyond thought and words. As Christ had two wills, there are two distinct kinds of love within Him,—the love which the Godhead ever had for its poor creatures, and the human love which He took upon Him as man. The only question is, how far did the one neutralize or destroy the other? Here is still the same dreadful Godhead; did it take away from the tenderness and affectionateness of the human Heart? or, did it take away from its power of feeling, while it imparted to it its dread unchangeableness?

In order to answer this question, we must go back to the principle laid down in the last chapter—that which took up into itself the Sacred Humanity was the Person of the Eternal Word. But while it elevated the Manhood, it destroyed nothing. What the Son of God assumed was a human heart, of the same nature as our own. Hope, fear, and love, the very elements out of which the matter of human passions is made, the self-same feelings which break out into lawless and disorganized affections, all were there. And if you ask how it is that in Jesus it produced no such result, the answer is the same as would be given in the case of the rest of mankind. Why is it that one man is cold, capricious, and selfish, while another is loving, gentle, and compassionate? Not because their natures are different, but because the persons, the responsible beings, composed of body and soul, use the powers of their common nature in a different way. The fire of the volcano is of the same matter as the flame which burns on our hearths, though the one destroys and the other cheers and warms us. Now, here is the Person of the Eternal Word acting on a human heart, with all the impulses, hopes, fears, affections, and desires of man. He takes away sin, nay, the very power of sinning; but all else He leaves as it was. He brings with Him the very purity of God, so that all that is wild and wayward is laid to sleep, while in its stead He brings from heaven a power of loving which no heart on earth ever possessed before. Since the Heart is human, its love is human too, but the intensity of it is ineffably increased by the power of the Person that elicits it.*

An act of love is the same in kind, breathed from the bosom of every child of Adam; but that it should come forth with all his heart, and with all the strength of his being is the result of the energy of the person who gathers up his whole power to produce it. No wonder, then, that the human Heart of Jesus should have within it a greater strength of love than the collective powers of all the Angels and Saints in heaven can produce. Each act of charity, as it issues from its inmost depths, has all the strength of God to heave it forth. Wherever fire is, it may not consume, but by the very power of its nature it must burn; and here the Godhead does not fuse the human Heart, but it makes it red-hot with love. The flame of its love is the same as ours, but the breath which fans it is the Spirit of the Everlasting Word. The whole power of Him, who

---

* According to the well-known maxim, Actus sunt suppositorum.

made the heavens out of nothing with a word, is turned to raising to its highest pitch the fiery furnace of a human heart. Each pulsation of its strong affections has the vehement rushing power of God the Son within it. As for the common love of man, its intensity is often in proportion to its lawlessness; while on the contrary, the pure spirit of an Angel can love, but it cannot feel. Here, in the Heart of Jesus, is all the feeling of man's nature without the wildness of its violence; here is the very purity of the Eternal Light, while the burning spirit of the Seraphim is but cold to the love which animates it. Oh! wondrous love of the virgin Heart of Jesus! It is not infinite, for it is created, and yet no Angel's plummet has ever sounded the depths of that illimitable ocean. Like the eternal love, it knows no progress, for it burned as vehemently at its first throb in the breast of the Infant Jesus as it does now in heaven. Pure as the uncreated Love, it burns for the race of man with the vehemence of a very passion. Strong with a Godlike strength, it is tender as a mother's.

Such is the influence of God upon His own human Heart; it reveals no new fact, it only brings home to us what we ought to have known before, that God is love. "Taste and see how sweet the Lord is," had been said of old, but now we know it, because that entrancing sweetness looks through human eyes, and melts in the tones of a human voice. Let us now fix our eyes upon the wonderful tenderness of the Heart of Jesus, remembering all the while who He is, and that if He be the most affectionate being that ever trod His own earth, it is because he is God. The depths of His soul are impenetrable, but we can guess at what went on within by its outward manifestations, so full of grace and truth. Let us now watch attentively all that the behaviour and actions reveal to us about the love of His Heart.

It is little enough which the Gospels tell us of the exterior of Jesus, but enough is known to show that the majesty of a sweet and winning love shone forth in all His actions. Born, as it was, of a virgin, formed in the womb of His mother by the direct action of the Holy Ghost, destined to be the organ of the most glorious soul that ever existed, we should have expected beforehand that the body of Jesus would be far more beautiful than even that of Adam in Paradise. Accordingly, the prophets foretold that He is to be beautiful exceedingly above the sons of men. And we have only to watch the effect of His appearance upon those around Him to see how, when in very deed He came on earth, a majestic sweetness shone in His very features, words, and gestures. He chose for his emblem the Lamb, the gentlest of creatures; and so deeply was it stamped upon His outward deportment, that the first exclamation of the holy Baptist, when he looked upon His face, was, Behold the Lamb of God. It was to have been expected in His infancy that sweetness should have been the characteristic of His looks. For if it be true that there ever shines in the eyes of childhood an innocent simplicity, unmixed, as yet, with the consciousness of reason, above all it would be so in those of the Infant Jesus, since He chose to pass through the years of infancy for the very purpose of winning us the more surely to Himself. He put on the look of childhood in its most winning form; quenching, of His own choice, the light of intellect in His infant eyes, that there might shine through them the more tenderly the playful liveliness of a mere child of earth. This was what might have been anticipated; but when He grew up and went forth into the world, see how the same characteristic of sweetness appears in every word, and deed, and look. He speaks but the word, and as He walks along the shore of the sea of Galilee, Apostle after Apostle leaves his all to follow Him. "Follow me," is all that He says, and they are His for life. Not only loving souls like that of St. John, or hearts full of zeal like that of St. Peter, were set on fire by a look or a word; whole crowds followed Him into the wilderness to hear Him speak. Wearied and tired, He had gone away into the desert out of very lassitude, when lo! He lifted up His eyes, and multitudes were seen moving in troops over the surface of the wild solitude. They left their homes; town and village were deserted. When once they had seen that beautiful face, and had heard the gracious words that fell from His sweet lips, He so fascinated them that they could not rest without Him. Without Him home is desolate, and with Him the desert blossoms like the rose.

No wonder, indeed, that they follow Him; the most hard-working missionary in the Church, St. Dominic, or St. Francis of Sales, is but a mere faint shadow of His unwearied sweetness. What a life was His during those three years of His ministry! By dawn of day He is in the temple; the gathering crowds find Him there; but they know not that He has had a journey already.* He has been upon the Mount of Olives, praying under the quiet, peaceful trees. His whole day has been mapped out already; He has foreseen the souls to whom He is to do good; the afflicted whom He is to comfort; the men and women whom He is to meet in the hot streets, the gracious words which He is to speak to the multitudes in the public places of the city. Or, if He quits Jerusalem, and goes up into Galilee, or passes through Samaria, there are weary journeys on foot, over hill and dale, on the dusty highway, or the savage wilderness. Wherever He comes to the habitations of men, on the village-green, or in the little hamlet hid in the mountains, He preaches. No time for rest or repose; a solitary woman comes to draw water from a well; He opens His parched lips, and speaks to her of the delicious spring of grace which He has within Him, and converts her. Or else He is by the sea-shore; the rude crowds

---

* "And Jesus went unto Mount Olivet, and early in the morning He came again into the temple."—John viii. 1.

press upon Him, and all but thrust Him into the waves. He embarks on the surface of the waters, and the prow of Peter's boat becomes His pulpit.

At least, you will say, there is the quiet night for rest; but Jesus has no house of His own; He has nowhere to lay His head. So tired is He that in the daytime He throws Himself on the deck of a fishing-boat, and out of very weariness lays His tired limbs on that hard couch, and sleeps. Yet often the night is spent on the bare ground, on the mountainside, with the dews of night wetting His garment and steeping His hair, in prayer for His poor creatures. Or else some Nicodemus comes to Him, and finds Him up and watching, for he chooses to have no time that He can call His own. Even when He slept, not even then did the constant Heart cease to love, or the mind to think about His creatures. It is of Him that it is said in the Canticles, I sleep, but my heart watches. His repose was not like ours, for it is said that even when His senses were laid to sleep, His consciousness was not suspended; and the acts of love for God and man which ever thrilled through His frame, went on as before. Yet with all this busy work, these nights spent in prayer, and days in toil, the gentle spirit never lost its balance, nor was its placid sweetness ruffled for a single moment.

Listen to His words, and you will hear how sweet they are. Wearied as He is with preaching, mothers bring their children to receive His blessing. His Apostles wish to send them away; they fear lest the importunity of childhood should tease Him, and exhaust His remaining strength; but He says, "Suffer the little children, and forbid them not to come to me." And he takes them up into His arms, and blesses them. The very quality which He holds out for universal imitation is this meekness and humility of heart, "Learn of me; because I am meek and humble of heart." Or, if you would know the winning power of His very glance, remember the effect of that one look which He cast on Peter. The Apostle was denying Him with an oath, when he met the eye of Jesus; and he immediately went out, and wept bitterly. It was at a moment when all dignity and beauty were gone from Him; His face was livid and swollen with blows, misshapen, and disfigured with blood; but the very sweetness of the Godhead was looking in gentle reproaches through those pleading, earnest eyes, and the repentant Apostle burst into tears. To his dying day, whenever the thought of that glance of Jesus came upon him, his tears began to flow anew.

But there is a greater test of character than such moments as that of the Passion; it is the intercourse of everyday life. Who could have told, beforehand, how God would behave among His creatures? How will the consciousness of Godhead act upon Him in the midst of the world? If he had shut Himself in a palace, like a king, and had shown Himself on some high holiday, surrounded with Angels for His guards, we might have imagined it. Or, if He had led the life of a hermit, wrapped up in perpetual contemplation, it would still have been conceivable. But throw Him upon the highway of life, take away even such a poor substitute for a cloister, as the prestige of riches or rank might give Him, make Him a public man, open to all by day or night: human imagination fails when it tries to picture to itself what would be the result. How will He demean Himself amid the rusticity of the poor, the unthinking selfishness of a crowd, the importunate curiosity of the intrusive, and the refined insolence of the rich? Yet there He is, from morning to night open to all, subjected to the arrogance of the Pharisee, the familiarity of the publican, the very gaze of the harlot. Rich and poor alike dare to invite Him to their houses. When a great man stoops to make companions of those who are beneath him, the perpetual thought of what is due to his dignity makes his condescension sit uneasily upon him. Jesus, however, is at home among all, down to the very publicans; while He bears unmoved the arrogant rudeness of the Pharisee. Nothing but the surpassing tenderness and sweetness of God could have moved so tranquilly amid all these difficulties.

But there is one test more, a greater one than all that has been noticed, and that is, the presence of sinners. When He comes into personal contact with public and notorious vice, when its victims are brought before Him in their character of sinners, surely then the purity of the Godhead, which destroyed Sodom and Gomorrha, will flash through the Manhood which it has assumed. The Pharisees bring before Him a woman taken in sin, and call upon Him to judge her. He first risks His life to save hers; He exposes Himself for her sake, to all the calumnies and misrepresentations for which His watchful enemies are sure to find a pretext in His clemency. And then when He is left alone with her, He releases her, and bids her go and sin no more.

Again; there is one wicked and notorious sinner who has come to hear Him, not out of a wish to be better, but because her sister Martha has talked her into it. She goes along the streets in the pomp and insolence of her beauty, the jewels glittering in her hair, throwing shameless glances around her, with sin in every look and every gesture. She is going to hear the Nazarene preach, and to defy His power. She comes within His influence, her looks are bent upon Him, and the sweet sound of His words reaches her ear. Oh! what a change comes over her! her eyes are riveted upon Him, and her color comes and goes. The tones of that voice have gone down to depths in her soul, of which she herself knew nothing. A moment ago she gloried in the triumph of her fascination, and exulted in her sinful power. Rich, noble, and young as she was, she could, especially in that ancient pagan world, set public opinion at defiance. Numbers as depraved as she, had shared the counsels and the friendship of the world's heroes and statesmen. But all at once there rises up before her a new thought for her, the degradation of sin. And then, with a crushing force, comes the view of God's dread justice, of death, and of eternity. She would have sunk to the earth had there not mingled with it, in the very depth of her horror and astonishment, the gentle hope of the mercy of God. Scared and frightened by these unwonted tumults, she rushes back to her home. Who could be the preacher that so strangely moved her? Who was the man that knew her soul so well? At the very sound of His voice light had flashed upon her mind, her trembling will had owned some mighty sway, and her proud heart had been crushed within her. Who could it be but God? She had heard of old of "God with us," of the mighty God who was to be born of a virgin; and, enlightened by divine grace, she felt that this must be He. She had seen her God, and yet, strange to say, guilty as she was, she felt no dismay; an unutterable love had taken possession of her soul, and she must see that heavenly countenance again. He could banish her forever, and well He might, considering what she was; but she must look upon the face of her God once more, if it were for the last time. She knew that He was to be at a banquet; her presence would be felt as a leprosy by all, but she cared not. What was the world to her now? So she cast off her silken robes, and put on her worst attire; and she took the jewels from her hair and trampled them under foot. With dishevelled locks flowing down her shoulders, and an alabaster vase of precious ointment in her hands, she walks rapidly through the streets to the house of the Pharisee. The guests stare wildly on her, as in this apparition, with pallid face and streaming hair, they recognise the Magdalene. But she sees no one but Jesus. All eyes are fixed on Him with greater wonder as she takes her station on her knees behind Him, as He lay reclining on the couch, according to the Roman custom. All think that He will shrink from her; but see, she grows bolder still, her lips approach His feet. Now surely He will rise and spurn her from Him. But, no, He bears the touch of her polluted lips, and the poor lost creature breaks her vase, and pours her ointment on His feet, while her bursting tears flow unrebuked upon them, and her long hair wipes off the moisture. Well may the Pharisee say in his scornful heart, This is no prophet, or He would have spurned her from Him. It is no prophet, but the omniscient God, He who had created and "called her by her name," who had "allured her and spoken to her heart." And now He turns His eyes upon her, and, amid the breathless silence of the spectators, the gentle tones of His voice bid them look upon "that woman," and proclaim aloud that because she loves Him she is forgiven.

Such is the way in which the lovingness of our God shows itself, when it takes a human shape, and concentrates itself in a human Heart. He has got a new organ for that love which He came on earth to kindle; and see how flames burst out from it on all sides. But human as it is in its tenderness, it is not human in its power and energy, nor in its constancy. The love which animates the breast of man has its progress and decay, its growth and decrease; it is ever apt to burn itself out by its own strength. But the love of Jesus cannot grow, because it is as great as possible at the very first, and burns unconsumed and undiminished to the last. "Having loved His own, He loved them to the end." He knew that

His time was come, and that He must go to the Father from whom He came; but His last thoughts are for them whom He is to leave on earth. What will they do when He is far from them? How will they bear the temptations and the misery of the world, when His presence is withdrawn, and He is seen no more on earth? Then it was that, in the depths of His loving wisdom, He devised a way by which He might be at once in heaven and on earth. The Blessed Sacrament was the last effort of His love, and when He had provided that His burning Heart should in very deed remain till doomsday on every altar in Christendom, He cheerfully went on His way to meet His cross.

Here we will leave Him for awhile, and pause to ask ourselves if ever there was love like this? And if our hearts and consciences tell us that never under human form was seen love at once so pure, so burning, and so constant, then let us call to mind that He who comes before us as the most tender and loving of beings is no other than our God. Let us remember the axiom with which we started; all this superabundant sweetness comes not in spite of, but out of His divine Person through His human nature. When God came down from heaven to become man, this was the form under which He chose to appear. He voluntarily chose to come as one who shed tears, and loved and felt human affection and misery. No one action of His Manhood was independent or involuntary. It was not independent, because the Godhead, by a distinct act, allowed it to take its own course, each time it wept, or bled, or loved. It was not involuntary, because the human will of man within Him, in its own natural way, melted into human tears, and loved with human love.

Now what could be the end and object of this unparalleled manifestation of love, except to win us to love Him in return? Why should God draw us "with the cords of Adam" if it were not to attract us to Himself, not with a dry, cold love, extracted from us by the word of command, but with the enthusiastic and affectionate love which belongs to man? We wish to love, and be loved in return, and Jesus, in assuming a human soul, took upon Himself this, its chief characteristic. No wonder, then, that throughout the history of the Church of God there has ever been this interchange of love between earth and heaven. The love of St. Cecilia, and of the dear martyr-child,

St. Agnes, offering up their young lives to Jesus, because "they would admit no lover but Him," are only the legitimate developments of Christianity; and the dilated heart and riven side of St. Philip are only the continuation of the same. Now is there any thing strange or inconsistent in the thought that the Jesus of the Gospels, who is the same forever, should manifest His love by giving His heart to St. Catherine of Sienna, and espousing her with a ring? There is nothing which need surprise, far less shock us, in the revelations made by our Lord about His Sacred Heart. When we hear of one who desires that we should call to mind His love under the symbol of a flaming heart, who would have men and women living in the world join themselves in confraternities to spread this love, what can we say but this, "It is the Lord?" Surely this is "one like the Son of man, who is alive and was dead, and behold He is living forever and ever."

CHAPTER IV.

THE LOVE OF THE HEART OF JESUS FOR SINNERS.

MUCH light has been thrown, by what has been already said upon the subject which we are considering. It has often been asked whether, when we speak of devotion to the Sacred Heart, we mean to honor the love which Jesus bore us, or the very heart of flesh and blood which was the organ of it. It now appears that the devotion takes in both together. We mean to worship our Lord's own real heart, and, at the same time, we take it as the symbol of His love. The Church uses human language, and assumes for her own purposes that common mode of speech, infinitely varied, and to be found in every nation under the sun, by which we employ the word "heart" when we would talk of love. Notwithstanding the different degree of susceptibility in the children of the sunny South, and of the stormy regions of the

North, the same phraseology runs through the rough, sonorous Teutonic, as well as the soft and feminine Tuscan. Nay, in no language does it occur in greater variety than in our own English tongue. Whether from this common witness of all languages we are right or wrong in inferring that that organ has more to do with human affections than any other, at all events it is quite sufficient for our purpose that such should be the common opinion of mankind. Jesus Himself has consecrated ordinary language with His own sacred lips, by speaking of Himself as "meek and humble of heart." In one word, then, the object of our adoration is the very Heart of Jesus, and the reason why we select it for adoration is, because it thrilled and palpitated with the emotions of His love, and like that of any other human being, is taken as the symbol of the joys, griefs, and affections, which in some way or other it really felt.

From all that has been said, it is plain that love may be said in general to be the spirit of the devotion to the Sacred Heart; and we are now in a condition to examine it with greater precision. In order to enable us to see it more clearly, let us try to explain what is meant by the genius of a devotion. Take any one of the objects of Christian devotion, the Mother of God, or the Blessed Sacrament, or the Precious Blood, of course there are ten thousand motives for honoring it. If, however, you look into the history of the honor paid to it, you will always find that some one, or more, of them comes out more prominently than the rest. Now these various motives may be said to be the form of the devotion, to constitute its genius, and the spirit which animates it.

At different times our Lord's Passion, for instance, may be looked upon as the cause of our Redemption, and so produce joy in us, or as unutterably painful to Himself, and so produce sympathy and compassion in us. According as these two different ideas come out as we contemplate the Passion, the devotion to it may be said to have a different spirit. This may be more clear in the worship paid to the Saints. If we were to be asked why one saint is honored in the Church more than another, we should probably answer, because he is more honorable; yet this would not be quite true. Consult theological writers, you will find that the Church, in assigning various grades of dignity to the saints whom she places on her altars, by no means pretends to settle the hierarchy of heaven. No, you must look elsewhere for the standard by which the Church classifies her saints. If you look into the character of each one of the great servants of God, specially raised up at certain periods of the Church, you will find that there is something in it peculiarly suited to the time at which he is made prominent. Now the devotion to him which lives after his death has a tendency to reproduce this character in those who love him, and to exercise a peculiar influence in Christendom. Surely, then, we cannot be wrong in assigning the instinct of the Church, by which she knows how far this character will suit her children's needs at a particular time, as one reason why she gives a greater prominence, and a greater solemnity to the worship of one saint than to that of another. For instance, it cannot be denied that in the first ages of the Church there appears a greater devotion to St. John the Baptist than to St. Joseph; now-a-days the very reverse is the fact. Why is this, if it be not because the worship of the Spouse of Mary, and the father of Jesus, is better suited to us than that of the mighty saint who was the herald of His coming? There is no jealousy in heaven, and the great St. John, the very apostle of disinterested love, would willingly point to St. Joseph and say, as he did to our Lord, "He must increase, and I must decrease." The thought of the sweet saint who guarded Jesus and Mary in their weary flight through the wilderness, was to be more useful to Christians than the remembrance of the stern voice which sounded through the desert. Devotion to St. Joseph breathes a different spirit from that which animates the devotion of St. John the Baptist. The reason why you love the one is utterly different from the motive which leads you to feel affection for the other. Again, the effect of that love on your own spiritual life is so completely distinct, that probably on looking back on God's past dealings with your soul, you might trace the changes in your inward life by the course of the various drawings toward particular saints in your heart. In other words, the devotion to each saint arises out of a different cause, and produces different results. It has a genius of its own.

Let us now pass on to consider the spirit of the devotion to the Sacred Heart of Jesus. Let us see what is the idea on which it is formed, and the effect which it is meant to have on our minds. And here I acknowledge myself at once to be at fault, not from the poverty, but from the very abundance of materials. The worship of any thing connected with our Lord's Manhood has this peculiarity, that its ultimate object is, as we have seen, the Person of the Eternal Word, and, therefore, however minute it may be, however it may confine itself to the smallest drop of His precious blood, or to the shortest moment of His existence, it has a bearing which carries you along in spite of yourself, you know not where. Above all, this is the case with His Sacred Heart; all other devotions resolve themselves into it. It is the fountain of the Precious Blood, and the red stream which issued from it drop by drop, during the Passion, found its way back at His resurrection to its old home, and animates it now in heaven. Again, as the spirit of this devotion is so intimately connected with the affections of Jesus, it has to do with every one of His actions from the womb of Mary to the grave, and on from them through His Easter life up into heaven at the right hand of God. Take life in any sense you will, it leads you straight to the Sacred Heart. It is the source of His bodily life; it is the centre of all that inward life, which may be called the Interior of Jesus. It rules over His infancy, it imparts a fire to the burning words of His sermons, and feeds the love of souls which kept up His sinking frame through the fatigue of His apostolic life. It smiles on His gracious lips, it lights up the love which He rains down upon sinners from His eyes, it weeps in the tears which spring up into them and drown their gentle lustre. Follow Him to heaven, and you will find it beaming and burning in the very centre of His glorified life. Nay, lift up the vail of His sacramental being, there it is again distinct and clear in the bosom of the living Jesus. Which, then, of all the devotions of which it may be the symbol, are we to take up, and which to exclude? Is the devotion to the Sacred Heart to trench upon that to the Infancy of Jesus, or to the Precious Blood, or to the Five Wounds, or, lastly, to the Blessed Sacrament? I answer that of course it may and does include them all, but it has, beside that, another spirit, peculiar to itself, and which can only be ascertained from Jesus Himself. Let us turn, then, to the visions to which I have so often referred, and we shall find in them what we cannot settle ourselves.

"One day when I was before the Blessed Sacrament exposed upon the altar, I felt an interior attraction, which gathered together within myself all the powers of my soul and all my senses. At that moment Jesus Christ, my divine Master, appeared before me all brilliant with glory, His five wounds resplendent as five suns. From His Sacred Manhood issued flames on all sides, but, above all, from His adorable breast, which was like a very furnace. In the midst of this burning furnace He showed me His loving heart, the source of all these flames. It was then that He explained to me the unspeakable wonders of His love, and showed me its exceeding power, since it made Him love men from whom He received nothing but coldness and ingratitude. 'It is that,' He said to me, 'which cuts me to the quick more than any thing I have suffered in my Passion. If they would but return me love for love, I should indeed think lightly of all that I have done for them. I would, if I could, do far more than I have done, but I receive from them nothing but coldness and affronts in return for all my eagerness to do them good.'"*

---

* Life of Ven. Margaret Mary Alacoque.

Here, then, we have distinctly stated what is the peculiar spirit of the devotion to the Sacred Heart. While the worship of the Five Wounds, or of the Precious Blood, points to the physical suffering of our Lord, and to the love which prompted them, that of the Heart of Jesus points to His inward woes, and, above all, to that overwhelming sorrow which came upon Him from the ingratitude of sinners to the end of time. It is the wailing melancholy complaint of Jesus that His Passion is forgotten, because men sin on, just as if He had never died for them. It is as if He could stand it no longer, and suddenly breaking through the vail which hides him from the visible world, came to reveal to a soul, which could sympathize with Him, how deeply His Heart had been affected by the neglect of those for whom He had shed His blood. It is plain then that if we would enter into the spirit of the devotion to the Sacred Heart, we must begin by contemplating the affections of that Heart toward sinners.

And now, if I had to put before you the spirit and the genius of the devotion to some of the saints of God, my task would be an easy one. I should have had simply to put before you his character. I should have studied the writings of his contemporaries and spiritual children, and, catching enthusiasm from them, have put together the minutest details of his features, his household words, and his every-day actions. I should have endeavored to draw a picture before you of the living and breathing man, with the look and bearing which he wore on earth; and I should have grouped around it the circumstances of the time, and the very scenery amid which he dwelt. I should very likely have failed; imagination would have come in, and I might have given you my view of the saint, which might or might not be the true one. Still no one could say that I was not doing what I had a right to do, because it was within the bounds of mortal power. But he would be a bold man who would dare to draw the character of Jesus. If any one attempted to do so, it requires no prophet to foretell that it would be a failure. Nay, let any one try to paint the character of the Blessed Virgin, I will answer for it that he fails. Your devout imagination, as you say your Rosary, may call up before you a beautiful image of your Mother. You may look into her gentle blue eyes, and fancy to yourself the sweet smile upon her lips, and hide your face in the folds of her mantle; but when it comes to the depths of her heart, who can enter into them? A man can take an individual joy or grief, and paint it as he best may; but when he comes to put them altogether, and to pass a eulogium upon her, as though he were making the panegyric of some saint, I defy him to succeed.

One reason of his failure may be this. The meaning of drawing a character in a work of fiction is, the bringing out some salient prominent quality, either good or bad, which predominates over the rest. Now when all the qualities are so well balanced, and every kind of temperament so well blended together, that nothing stands out beyond the rest of the being, of course it is impossible even to attempt the task. This is, however, but one, and perhaps the very least of the reasons which would deter a wise man from undertaking a portrait of the Mother of God. What, then, must it be in the case of God Himself? There is a legend that a painter mingled with the crowd about Jesus, and attempted to draw a likeness of His face. But such was the flashing lustre of His eye, and the changeful majesty, mingled with sweetness of His features, that the rash artist felt that he was baffled, and withdrew in despair. This is but a feeble image of the folly of those who have attempted to make out for themselves the peculiar character of our Lord; so miserably have they failed, that those who, forgetting that he was God, have undertaken the task, have at length discovered some imperfections in Him, and have ended by preferring some of His creatures to Him. They have thought that they could construct an ideal far more heroic, more generous, and more godlike than that which God has raised.

Far be it from us to attempt what can only lead to discomfiture and defeat. Imagination must look for another subject-matter to exercise herself upon; and as for the intellect, it would turn to folly if it tried to clothe in words what is too deep for ideas, and defies the range of human calculus. Yet it is absolutely necessary for us to enter into the feelings and affections of Jesus, if we would have any notion of the genius of the devotion to His Sacred Heart. One thing, then, remains for us to do, and that is, to follow the theologians of the Church, and the visions of the saints, in what they have told us about the Interior of Jesus. Without venturing to draw out His character, we can, with the help of many a monk of old, after diving into many a too-neglected folio, attempt to draw out before you the love of the Heart of Jesus. And we will walk with a firm step, though ours is no less a task than to analyse the structure of the Sacred Manhood, to adjust its parts together, and to show especially the relation in which His affections stand to the rest of His being. We will not fear, for the blessed St. Thomas is going before us to guide our feeble steps, and we will call upon the Heart of Mary to help us, while we enter into the very depths of the affections of the Incarnate Word, and trace out the part which they bore in the workings of that glorious Manhood, by which He redeemed the world.

Nor need you fear lest I should lead you beyond your depth into discussions fit only for the schools. St. Philip would be angry with me if I did so; but he will only smile, and help both you and me to enter more deeply into the Sacred Heart, if for the glory of God, and out of very love for Jesus we do our best to understand Him, that we may love Him more. St. Philip does not forbid scholastic subjects, else he would exclude all theology, and reduce his sermons to moral essays; he only forbids their being treated scholastically.

Come, then, we will endeavor to enter upon this great subject: and that the discussion may not be vague and aimless, let us remember that it bears directly upon the Sacred Heart. Our object is to discover to what extent it is true that Jesus felt human affections and human feelings. In the vision which has been read to you, He complains bitterly, like a man who is hurt at ingratitude, and at the same time feels a burning love for those very ungrateful sinners, and a deep sorrow for their everlasting ruin. Now, are these expressions the exaggerated offspring of a pious imagination, or are they the real truth? The question is a most important one, for I do believe that one reason why men sin on is, because, from the very vastness of the powers employed, they are unable to realize the inward sorrows of the crucifixion. They look upon it as a vast drama, in which God shows His justice, a wonderful scene of blood and of agonizing pain, so stupendous that it is beyond them. I do believe that they repeat to themselves in their secret hearts: "Aye, it is God who suffers," till at last a sort of silent corollary follows, "therefore He can bear it." The tenderness and the touching affectionateness of Jesus escapes them. Again, when a man has sinned, and sin has become an overmastering habit, so that he says and believes that he cannot help sinning, then a fearful temptation comes over him to look upon the Passion and the crucifixion as not meant for him. The periodical recurrence of the wicked act, and the fiend-like power of temptation are dread realities. His languid will has already bent hundreds of times before the mighty influence; and in all human probability, when the time comes, it will bend again, and so on without a term. What a temptation to the poor soul, to say that Jesus does not love him, that he cannot help sinning! Now the answer given to this devil's logic by the Sacred Heart is just this; he can help sinning, for Jesus has not only suffered outwardly, but has felt for him. In one word, sinners have no notion whatever how Jesus loves them, and saints have only a faint idea of it; Mary knows something of it, but only because her heart is akin to the Heart of Jesus. Once more, then, how far is all this true?

Now, then, turn your eyes upon the Manhood of Jesus. I grant you it is hard enough in the superhuman structure of His being, to discover any thing like an entrance for grief or for the weakness of human feeling. Of course, I am speaking now of His humanity, apart from His Godhead. Though the two are joined together in one Divine Person, yet you know well that each has its separate powers. The Manhood has its own intellect and will, and the Godhead does not interfere with either. Again, the human intellect does not see by means of the divine; it has its own workings and its own thoughts, as the will has its own love. For all the everlasting knowledge of the Eternal Word, the human understanding might be dark and ignorant if God had chosen it, for the two are perfectly distinct. But, oh! for all that, what a flood of light upon that mighty intellect! what unutterable and appalling strength! To understand it we must call to mind what has been said, and add something more. There was no need, it is true, of sanctifying grace to make it holy. Every other being except the Godhead, even Mary herself, is holy with a sanctity which is within it, but not of it. But as for the Sacred Humanity, even if no one ray of grace from heaven ever found its way upon it, it would still be holy with a boundless holiness, since what sanctifies it is the Person of the Eternal Word, which is its own. At the same time, that all in this wonderful being may be in harmony and keeping, and lest there should be some jar or recoil in the workings of it through the disproportionateness of the powers in action, sanctifying grace is given to it, in addition to the sanctity which it had already. God rained down upon it a created beauty, over and above what was absolutely necessary for it. You may estimate how great it was when you are told that the very object of it was to raise the human powers so high that the Person of God might work through them, as a fitting instrument, obedient, but not inanimate. Sanctifying grace was given to the Manhood to give it some proportion to the Eternal Word which was one with it, and to strengthen its powers lest they should quiver and tremble beneath the hand which used them.* It seems an idle thing to talk of quantity in

---

* Dicendum quod humanitas Christi est instrumentum Divinitatis non quidem sicut instrumentum inanimatum, quod nullo modo agit, sed solum agitur; sed tanquam instrumentum anima rationali animatum quod ita agitur, quod etiam agit. Et ideo *ad convenientiam actionis* oportet eum habere gratiam habitualem. St. Thomas, Summa, 3, 7, Art. 1, Ad. 3. See also Suarez de Incar. Disp. 18, Sect. 2.

grace, as though it could be measured by an earthly standard; but let us try to attain to some idea of it. You know that, to estimate how much was given to Mary, you are told to imagine, if you can, in thóught, all the graces of the saints in paradise, and then to add the powers of the angelic spirits, from Michael to the lowest angel of them all. Yet, after all, you are told that put together they are as nothing to those which God has given to His blessed Mother. These seem to you wild words, but I tell you that you must add on Mary's portion to all this, and yet your weak arithmetic must own itself baffled, for you will not have reached the sum of the graces given to the Manhood of Jesus. They are only not infinite, because grace is a created thing, and so God was forced to stop somewhere.

Now, then, turn to the intellect of Jesus; here, again, you have strength unutterable, without any mixture of weakness. As though one was not enough, three several sorts of knowledge were given to it.* First of all, conceive, if you can, an active energizing intellect, without the ignorance and the dim-sightedness which

---

* St. Thomas, Summa, 3, 8, passim.

we get from Adam. Imagine it starting from a point where the greatest genius upon earth would be too proud to end, and then storing up within itself, in addition, by experience, as we do, the knowledge of all bright things in heaven and in earth. Yet think not that any thing in this outward world could be a novelty to Him, even though it met His eye for the first time; for, besides this human knowledge which we have noticed, even before He saw the light there had come upon His soul an image of each several thing in this vast universe, such as the angels had from their birth, not derived from sense, but poured into them, a bright and glowing impress from the mind of God. Here, then, was already power of intellect enough, even if there were nothing more, to furnish forth a host of cherubim in heaven. Then, in addition to all, remember that from the first moment of His life, in the dark womb of Mary, during His smiling infancy, as He walked a full-grown man on the borders of the blue lakes of Palestine, nay, when His eye was swimming in the agonies of death upon the cross, there was ever before His mind, not the dim vision, but the rapturous sight of the real Godhead. There it was ever before Him, and such a measure of it, that the sight of God vouchsafed to all the beatified spirits in heaven, was but darkness compared to it. There it was in His inmost soul, with all that it involved, the past without beginning, and the passing present, and the future without end. In consequence of this beatific vision all the souls and spirits that ever were, or that ever will be, with all their several thoughts, words, and deeds, came thronging in one vast, clear, distinct view, before His mind.

Oh! what a soul was this, vast and comprehensive enough to take in at one view all that is, and was, and is to come. At the same time it was clear-sighted and minute enough to know their smallest details, so that the life of each being lay before it, all disentangled from the rest, and ready for the day of judgment. It could call before itself all the glories of dead empires, with their bygone crimes; while at one glance it could look abroad upon the living earth, as it swings in mid-heaven, and hurries on to its doom, with its roar of huge cities, and its still solitudes, its lonely forests and its mighty seas, all lying in heat or in shade, in storm or in calm, basking under the broad glare of day, or bathed in the cool radiance of a cloudless moon. I say nothing of the deepening abyss of countless stars in heaven, nor of the angelic hosts with their nine choirs above, because beyond all there is a deeper depth; for in the mind of God there is a boundless store of worlds, which might be, and never will be. This beautiful universe is but a specimen of His creative power, and lovely as it is, there are thoughts enough in the intellect of God to call forth myriads of worlds, filled with beings, each brighter and more lovely than the angels and the saints. Now the knowledge of all these forms another science by itself, distinct from any other; and so you must place in the mind of Jesus, over and above what we have named, not a full understanding, for that cannot be without raising His human soul to the rank of Godhead, but a partial vision of what may be called this poetry, this silent music in the mind of God.*

And now we may form some estimate of the greatness of the intellect of Jesus. Its stores of knowledge are all but boundless, its field of vision is all but infinite, and it is peopled with

---

* Horum quædam sunt in sola potentia divina, et hujusmodi non omnia cognoscit in Verbo anima Christi. S. Thomas, Summa, 3. 16. 2.

objects which are simply numberless. Oh! what a strength must there have been in that human soul to manage all these wondrous treasures, to keep them all apart and distinct, to gaze, without being dazzled, upon this incomprehensible abyss of deepening light. One vision, far short of the beatific, is enough to throw into ecstasy a saint of God. St. Philip walked about like a man from the grave, with a ghost-like whiteness on his face, after one glimpse of the invisible world. But Jesus did not stagger under this superincumbent weight of glory, and had power enough to walk calm and upright, and to go about His actions like an ordinary man. Oh! happy being, lofty intellect, soul not aspiring, for it could go no higher, but bathed in unutterable floods of glory. As He stands like a giant ready to run His resistless race, it would be hard, indeed, to find within Him any thing that looks like an inlet for weakness.

We have gone a considerable way already, but still there is one whole branch of the subject to be considered before we arrive directly at the Sacred Heart, and that is the human will of Jesus. Here, too, you find capacities for happiness such as never were in any other being. Beatitude is its natural state; it was born with it. Then, again, just like God, that blessed Manhood, as we have already said, cannot sin. It needs no grace, like every other being, even the angels and Mary herself, but it has within itself, the Person of the Eternal Word, which is its own, which rules and guides its will. It has thus a self-sufficing purity which makes it pure with a spotlessness, to which angelic cleanness is but corruption, the very Purity of God. Oh! who can tell the joys of that virgin bosom, with the whole of its fiery capacity of love turned upon God? Send Him forth into the world, that sinless Lamb; surely pain can but touch His limbs, it will not reach His heart. As far as we have seen as yet, we might argue that His mind was beyond the reach of sorrow. Men may nail Him to a cross, but at least we might infer that His soul will remain in undisturbed repose since it is all the time floating in the joys of the beatific vision. Above all, for we have come to it at last, happy beyond thought must be the blessed Heart of Jesus, the very centre of this mighty being, ruling with gentle sway this empire of love, and crowned king of all His powers. Oh! how blissful must be the Heart of Jesus.

since it is inseparably united to the Eternal Word, and born in the very fires of the Holy Spirit, so that its every throb is an heroic act of the love of God.

Happy, indeed, it would be with a bliss without alloy, if besides charity for the everlasting God, it had not had another love, and that was a boundless love for man. As yet in every portion of the soul of Jesus which we have considered, we have found nothing but strength unmingled with weakness, and happiness impregnable to the attacks of sorrow. But here at length we have come to a part which may serve for an inlet, by which the waters of bitterness may find their way to His inmost soul. Amid all this strength He chose that His Heart should be left vulnerable on purpose that He might suffer. And that you may understand this, you must remember that the same was the case with the body of Jesus. Its appropriate condition, so to speak, would have been a glorified state even upon earth. In other words, though it was a body of flesh and blood, yet as it was elevated to be the flesh of the Eternal Word, it would have been convenient that it should share the beatification of the soul. But He willed that it should remain the same weak suffering thing, as all other bodies inherited from Adam. He chose that its transfiguration should be but a passing state, in order that it might suffer and die upon the cross. In the same way, while the upper portion of His soul was filled with the joys of the beatific vision, that heavenly joy was bidden to stop short of the lower part of His spiritual nature. Now if you remember that in this lower part of the human soul is fixed the seat of grief and of fear, and of all the agitating feelings which chill, cast down, shake, and pierce the heart of man, you are at once able to understand how His Sacred Heart lay exposed to all that man, or devil, or God Himself might inflict upon it. He had but to give the word Himself, and floods of strange and unknown sorrows might at once be let in upon it. While the depths of His soul were lying motionless in unutterable calm, the surface of it might, at His own bidding, be the sport of all the storms of hell.

Now, then, send into the world this wondrous being, and let Him make His way in it as He can. Gift Him with all this mighty intellect, with a godlike will, and a firmness of purpose, which not all hell can move, yet you have left one vulnerable point, and that is His Sacred Heart. Can you prophecy how that Heart will fare on its journey through the world? You cannot tell beforehand; it simply depends upon Himself, for all His feelings are so perfectly under the command of His Divine Person, that it must give them leave before they can begin to stir. The only way to ascertain the question, then, is to see not what He might have done, but what he actually did. Now we have already seen that of all the gentle loving hearts that ever bled or wept on earth, the Heart of Jesus was the most tender and the most affectionate. Yet there are other things, which we have not noticed yet, and which prove how His heart had all the characteristics of ours in it.

He goes through the world as though God was not enough for Him; He longed for the love of man. That virginal Heart was ready to throw its affections away on objects unworthy of it. A young man comes and asks the way to heaven, and "Jesus loves him." Is not His heart evidently nourished from the breast of Mary, and framed out of her own best heart's blood? nay, is it not more tender and compassionate than His very Mother's?

With what a mighty love, yet how familiar and affectionate, did it love the disciple who lay upon His bosom, and heard its beatings. And if there is one thing which approaches to a distinctive character in Jesus, it is that He was sensitive, by which I mean, that His heart keenly felt neglect and ingratitude. Take but one scene of His earthly life. There was an hour of overmastering agony, when the very fiends of hell were doing their worst upon Him. See by the light of the Paschal moon the prostrate form arises, and bends over His three disciples, and, oh! with a touching melancholy cry, He goes back to His prayer, like a disappointed man, because His very friends had left Him to His lonely struggle, and cared not for Him in His utmost need. Three times he comes to seek for sympathy, and the third, as He emerges from the deep shadow of the olive-trees, His face is ghastly pale, and there are crimson beads of blood upon His brow, to show us how He feels the indifference of His friends.

It is this sensitiveness, as I have called it, of His Heart to ingratitude, which according to our measure enables us to enter into His agony. Let us remember that a love for sinners may be said to have been His ruling passion. At the same time we must call to mind something more about the human will of Jesus. It had, first of all, a perfect and entire conformity to the will of God which it knew, because it saw it. On the other hand, there was left in His lower will a power, not of resisting God's will, but of desiring what is never to be, and of clinging to it up to the very point where it would begin to be sin or imperfection to desire it. If we put all this together, it is easy now to calculate what would be the result of sending into the world the gentle tender-hearted being whom we have described. Remember there is pent up within the narrow boundary of His Heart a fiery love for souls, a burning desire of saving all, embracing every man and woman in every age and in every country. Do not forget to throw into the account that this love in His Heart is neither more nor less than the love of God for the creatures that He has made. Then set Him on His bended knees, praying to the Eternal Father, that He might not have the agony of seeing His children perish forever. Lastly, suppose that, instead of the gentle moon looking down from heaven upon the whispering trees, there rises before Him in that dark valley the very pit of hell, and its hungry flames fed with the flesh and blood of those for whom He had been praying. Imagine that the prayer is still waxing hotter and hotter, while God still rejects it, because they choose to rush upon their own destruction and to sin; is it any wonder, then, that His Heart, in the torment and the torture of this strong desire unsatisfied should, in the very beginning of His Passion, break out into a sweat of blood?

Ah! dreadful witness to the reality of the feelings of the Heart of Jesus. Well, indeed, has He earned the right to represent Himself to the end of time in visions to His saints as the Man with the bleeding Heart. He had suffered in very deed in His agony for the ingratitude of sinners living on earth at the time, that He appeared with lacerated Heart in visions to His Saints. Think of what has been said of His intellect; you will see that the wounds to be inflicted on its sensitiveness by sinners, till the day of judgment, were anticipated and crowded into those moments spent in the garden of Gethsemane. Then and there arose before Him the sins not of a single night or a single town, but of a world through the long course of ages, every moment of which brings forth its separate sin. The great Creator looks abroad in spirit over the earth which He has made. In heaven he can wrap Himself up in His dread unchangeableness, but He has come in human flesh, and with a human soul, which can feel, and love, and shed tears of blood over the fate of His creation. The history of the world is before His mind, past, present, and to come; and He must needs show us, once for all, what a mighty grief its funeral deserves. Time and space are swept away from His mind, and He sees all human beings at a glance. They are all there, godlike creatures whom He had borne in His everlasting womb for all eternity, whom He yearns for now with a human heart. He knows them all by their names, but now He can only look in helpless agony upon the progress and the issue of their guilt. He looks into the inmost soul of each, and sees it torn with horrid passions, with thirst for gold, or the lust of empire, or all on fire with unholy love, pallid with rage, or withering away with jealousy and hate. His intellect is thronged and peopled with the miserable forms of sinners, the tyrant and the oppressed, the midnight murderer, the seducer and his prey; and He, with His boundless love for them, is looking all the while into their hearts, and seeing how they are obstinately bent on their own ruin. He could not save them, because they would not; His very prayers only gave them new graces to abuse, and His very presence increased their present guilt and their future pain.

Ah! why did not His Father in His mercy spare Him the sight? Why did He not spare Himself? Why not give Him an intellect less far-seeing, or else a heart less vulnerable and less loving? Why wed together such gigantic strength of intellect, as to see into the very pit of hell, with affections so easily moved and so persevering? Why give Him charity so ardent, yet lodge it in a Heart of such delicate texture that while it cannot bear ingratitude it must needs love the sinner, so all-embracing that it will fasten itself with a strange tenacity on the filthiest souls, and pour out upon the most impure the unutterable treasure of His tender love? Alas! poor Heart of Jesus, it is the victim of all; all conspire against it. The intellect shows it on the one hand, the horror of sin, and, on the other, the majesty of God prepared to destroy it. The will in its immovable strength gives them up to God because their doom is just; and all the while the Heart is weak enough to love such wretched creatures with a strength of love which is a very torment to it. Why not save them then? But they will not be saved. What, then, can it do, but fly to the welcome cross and shed its last drop of blood, and pour it all out in one concentrated act of love for all mankind, whether they will be saved or no? Alas! poor heart it would fain prolong its torture forever and ever. Jesus would hang there till the day of judgment; but He knows the hearts of men too well. He has had too much experience of their black ingratitude not to know that it would be useless. Why, men are sinning at the very foot of His cross; there is a hardened wretch by His side, on His left hand, blaspheming with his dying breath. No, the Heart of Jesus has done all it could. It can do but one thing more, it can only break. Oh! there was life enough still in His mangled form to have lived on upon the cross. His last cry was a mighty voice, which showed how He might have borne His agony for hours more all through the livelong night. But His weary

Heart could bear no part, and so He died of a broken Heart for the sins of men.

And now that all is over, and that loving Heart is still, let us come calmly and look upon the work of our hands. The sun has gone down upon Jerusalem, and the moon, which witnessed yesterday the faint droppings of His blood, now throws its pale light upon the group which prepares Him for His funeral. He lies motionless in His Mother's lap, and His lips are mute; He could not reproach you if He would; and she can only point with silent finger to the wound in His side, and show you how it pierced His Heart. Yet there is a silent eloquence in that gaping wound, which tells you more than words can express. It tells you that the Crucifixion was no mere exhibition of the power and justice of God; but a proof of the real and hearty desire of the Creator to save His creatures. It is the voice of Jesus, saying, "It was due to me that the manhood which I assumed should be more glorious than the angels. I might have come down with seraphic face, reflecting the unutterable bliss of my beatified Heart. By right my Body should have been glorified, and my Heart beyond the reach of woe. But instead of that

I came upon earth with a body vulnerable as your own, and a soul more vulnerable still. My Heart is filled with the tenderest love for every sinner of you all; and in proportion to its tenderness, it is in peril of being torn by all who choose to lacerate it. If you are lost at last it is no fault of mine; can you doubt that I do my best to save you, since I died brokenhearted at the thought of the everlasting doom of my wretched creatures?"

If, then, you would know in a few words the genius of the devotion to the Heart of Jesus with respect to sinners, I would simply say that it is the complaint of Jesus that men will be lost, though He does all He can to save them. At the same time it is a gracious expedient of the love of our Blessed Lord, protesting that, to the last, He is ready to receive them, and that His Sacred Heart in Heaven beats with the same love for them as it did at the moment of His death.

CHAPTER V.

THE LOVE OF THE HEART OF JESUS FOR THOSE WHO ARE AIMING AT PERFECTION.

WE have already advanced a long way in our task, so long, that if we did not remember that the subject on which we are employed is the love of Jesus for man, we might suppose that our labour was over. But who can measure the height and depth, the length and breadth of the charity of God? Beyond all that we have gone through, there is a deeper depth, which we have to sound before we have done. As yet we have seen the mercy of God, flooding the earth, as the waters cover the sea, but we have only skimmed its surface. There are still unutterable treasures of love in that vast ocean, of which we have said nothing. It would be a great mistake to suppose that mercy for sinners is the only attribute of God displayed in the Passion. Accordingly in the Heart of Jesus, the faithful organ with which the Eternal Word obeyed His Father's will, there is a love more fiery than that which burned for sinners. It is His love for those who are aiming at something more than the lives of ordinary Christians, and are doing their best to become Saints. It is certain that these same souls burn with a greater love of God than others, since, not content with scant measures of grace, they wish to sacrifice all for God, without stopping at what is barely necessary to get to heaven. It is, therefore, only natural to suppose that Jesus, on His side, loves them even with a greater love than He loves those whose salvation is in greater danger because of their state of sin. It is no wonder, then, if His Sacred Heart has a special message for them, nor that it is necessary to devote some time to the consideration of the spirit of this devotion, as intended for those who are going on to perfection.

We will then quit the distressing scene which we have witnessed, souls redeemed by Jesus, turning a deaf ear to all His entreaties, even while He, with unabated love, is expending the treasures of His Heart upon them. It will be a joyful thing to rise above the thick and murky atmosphere through which the cries of the mighty battle between good and evil are struggling up to heaven, and to advance into the kingdom of grace, where Mary is Queen, and where Jesus reigns. Thanks be to God there is still many a soul on which the Heart of Jesus reposes, without being ever dislodged from His throne. Negative sinlessness, even if it were possible, would be but a poor specimen of the realms of grace; and beyond the common ordinary Christian life there is a great creation of Almighty God, hierarchy upon hierarchy of souls, rivalling in their beauty, order, and variety, those of the very angels in heaven. Men make a wonderful mistake when they confine their notions of the world of grace to the ordinary phenomena which lie upon its surface. An infidel falls into a fatal error when he looks upon naked human nature, steeped as it is in original and actual sin, as the fairest ideal of the race of men. He gets a miserable view of God's glory, who looks upon this earth, with its imperfect justice and triumphant vice, as the whole of the moral system of the universe. He forgets the unseen world, the deep cauldron of hell, with its living fire, and the penal flames of purgatory, and above all the calm majestic heaven peopled with saints and angels, and illuminated by the glory of Mary and the beaming wounds of Jesus. And a similar error it is to bound the results of Christianity to the mere orderly, respectable Catholics in a state of grace, forgetting that the genuine fruits of the Passion are the saints of God, and all in their measure who are aiming at serving God in the path of evangelical perfection.

Thanks be to God, it seems to be one of the characteristics of the times in which we live, that the class of Christians to which we refer seems more widely diffused than at any other age of the Church since primitive times. In the middle ages, for instance, perfection was all but coextensive with the cloister. Any one acquainted with the history and letters of the great St. Bernard will see that his tendency was to consider that salvation in that mediæval world was the very outside which could be hoped for; while any thing resembling a perfect life was the wildest of dreams beyond the walls of a monastery. He bids his nephew, with the whole energy of his impassioned eloquence, flee from Cluny if he would save his soul; how much more from the world? It is not, however, necessary to go so far back as the twelfth century to prove this point. We have only to fix our eyes on the history of the period of transition from mediæval to modern times, in order to be sure that a change has taken place. Compare, for instance, the rules of the Oratory of Divine Love, of which St. Cajetan and Cardinal Pole, in his youth, were members, and which was expressly formed for men living in the world, with those of its successor, St. Philip's Little Oratory. In the former case the rule prescribed communion four times a year to the brethren; while in the case of the Oratorium Parvum, the brethren are required to communicate once a month, at least, and they are recommended to approach the Sacraments once a week, and our Lady's feasts. It is evident that in the interval between the formation of the two societies, both intended for persons who had no vocation for the cloister, the standard of religious attainment possible for those living in the midst of society, had been very much raised. Again, the preface of a book no more recondite than the Introduction to a Devout Life, suffices to prove that the sweet St. Francis of Sales effected for France what St. Philip Neri had done for Italy.

It is not a mere fancy, then, if we consider that the Christian's life in these days of ours resembles rather the primitive ages of the

Church than the more romantic beauty of mediæval times. Like the early Christians we too are flung into the midst of a form of society, the very frame and structure of which is anti-christian. Yet just as in Rome and Antioch of old the Christian virgin did not leave her home or fly to a cloister which as yet had no existence, so now it is often in the very midst of the turmoil and restlessness of modern civilization that God finds His own, who are doing their best to love Him with all their heart. It is quite true that the cloister is the natural home of those who wish to give up all for Christ; still it is a consolation for Christians whose vocation is to be in the world, to think that perfection is not impossible for them It would be a miserable thought, if it were true that to be in the world is necessarily to be of it. To those whose duties lie there, it may be a comfort to remember the days of old, when St. Cecilia and St. Agnes were living in the midst of Roman life, yet daily feeding on the Body and Blood of their Spouse. So now also it is an established point that frequent communion is not to be denied to those who live in the world, provided that their hearts are unworldly, and they are aiming at being saints.

There is no rank or station in life, therefore, to which a devotion to the Sacred Heart is unfitted, though it originally took its birth in the cloister, since there is no single grade of society in which some may not be found who are doing their best to aim at perfection. And what devotion is more fitted for them than that, the very aim and object of which is to adore the inward life of love of that Heart of Jesus, and to sympathise with His life-long hidden woes, even before ever the scourge and cross had wrung a drop of blood from Him? In like manner all they can do for Him is in their turn to love and suffer in secret, while outwardly they are like the rest of the world. It is no one outward act of Jesus that is commemorated here, but the whole burning love which prompted all His actions from the first moment of His earthly being in Mary's womb, to the last sigh which he breathed upon the cross. Now, love is the beginning and end of this devotion, and if they can do nothing else, at least their whole lives will be one long holocaust of love, even though, like St. John, the first disciple of the Sacred Heart, no outward martyrdom enable them to shed their blood for Christ.

But there is one especial message conveyed

to such suffering souls from the Heart of Jesus, one which they especially need, namely, an exhortation to boundless confidence in His love. If there be one thing more than another which stands in the way of those who are aiming at perfection, it is the discouragement which perpetually seizes upon them at the sight of their own failings and short-comings. "Can God love such a creature as I am?" is the ever-recurring question which the heart asks itself, when at the close of each day the same miserable tale of littlenesses and imperfections comes before it. It is not too much to say that a bitter sense of disappointment but too often comes over those who have given themselves to God. Look at those who, it may be, first gave themselves to Him with a generous spirit, enough to make apostles of them, and thought that now nothing was before them but a life-long cheerful sacrifice for God. Look at them a few years after; how often are they found sick of the weary struggle, ready to ask themselves whether their early aspirations were, after all, more than a dream of a devout imagination. It is at such times as these that the very Cross and the Precious Blood of Jesus seem to frighten us, for of what do they tell us but of high heroic sacrifice, and of fortitude such as shames our weakness? It seems as though there was no place beneath the cross except for virgin souls, like Mary or St. John, or else for the Magdalen's burning love, or the broken-hearted contrition of the repentant thief. Oh! what a joy it is at that moment of dreary darkness, to fix our thoughts upon the Heart of Jesus, on its tender suffering, and the boundless love which animated every action of His life! It was when we were sinners that He first loved us, out of His gratuitous love, and He will not leave us now in spite of all. Nay, more than this, if we look into the Heart of Jesus, we shall find that in His Passion He has chosen to suffer even down to the very weaknesses and repugnances of our nature, in as far as they were not sin. He will compassionate the very feebleness of our lower will, since He Himself, in His thoughtful love has chosen to feel it for us. He has taken upon Himself to be the universal Victim for human nature, and He would but represent it ill, if there was any grief incident to a human soul, of which His tender suffering Heart had not borne the brunt.

Since such is the spirit of the devotion to the Sacred Heart of Jesus, it will be well to devote this chapter to the special consideration of this wonderful union of strength and weakness, which forms as it were the characteristic of His life and sufferings. It will lead us to inquire more deeply into the mysteries of His being, the glorious sanctity of His manhood, the various operations of its will, and its unshaken resolve, united with the most touching tenderness of affection, and all the varying emotions of a human heart. It is to the same garden of Gethsemane that we should betake ourselves, in order to see this new phase of the sufferings of the Heart of Jesus. Hitherto we have looked upon the strength of the love of the Sacred Heart; now we shall enter upon another branch of the subject, and inquire into the cause of its repugnances. It will furnish an answer to the temptation, which especially assaults the soul on the difficult path of perfection. There is a period in the spiritual life, when the consciousness of its weakness comes upon it with a dreadful force. Confidence in self is the first thing which it has to unlearn, and when it first discovers that it cannot do any thing which it aspires to, that on the contrary it can do nothing by itself, its consciousness of impotence fills it with shame and terror, and tends to separate it from God. It cannot understand how Jesus can be a model for it, except by the merest fiction, if the strong and mighty Person of the Word overmastered all difficulties, without a struggle, and never felt the pain and the uneasiness caused by the infirmities of the human will. The soul even shrinks from the very Heart of Jesus, till it learns that that Sacred Heart had its weakness too. Jesus chose to suffer our infirmities, not to encourage us in weakly yielding to them, but to show us how to overcome them, and to urge us on to seek a support for our weakness in the sympathies of His Sacred Heart. In order to show this, we will now enter upon the consideration, first, of the inherent strength of the will of Jesus; secondly, of its apparent vacillations, and its repugnances to suffer in the garden of His agony.

Come, then, let us go forth and see our King crowned with the diadem with which His mother crowned Him in the day of His joy and triumph. Mary's consent has been given; the Virgin has conceived, but the Archangel's tongue is too poor to herald forth the praises of her child. Who can proclaim the style and title of this mighty King? Creature He cannot be called, although He has a created nature, for He is the very God who made the heavens. The highest of the Seraphim is, after all, but the mere servant of his Creator; but here is one who is man, yet cannot be called the servant of God, since He is His only-begotten Son. Wonderful indeed is that child who is born sovereign of the universe; but more wonderful still, because, though He be the King of Kings, He finds Himself bound by a vassalage which makes Him the slave of all. Hear Him speak of Himself, and He will say, "I am a worm, and no man, the reproach of men, and the outcast of the people." You might imagine that the career of this bright and glorious being must be one continual series of triumphs, that His soul must be ever like a cup, filled to the brim with joy; but watch Him, and all at once, in the strength and the beauty of His manhood, you find Him prostrate on the ground, His face pallid, and His Heart throbbing with fear. Nay, more, the depths of His soul are stirred, and there is a struggle going on within Him. Oh! who can have overthrown this powerful conqueror, and uncrowned this mighty King? What elements of war can there be within Him, that all at once peace should have departed from His calm and majestic spirit? The only way to solve the question is this: He has made Himself the Victim for the human race, and He must suffer all that man can suffer. The universal groans of the miserable race of man have been heard in heaven, and God has come down Himself to suffer with them. And to show them how human He was in His suffering, He must needs take upon Himself the very weakness of sorrowing man. As usual, His Sacred Heart is the first to bear the penalty. It was the seat of this mighty agony; and we shall never understand either the nature of the contest, nor the unutterable love of Jesus for man, until we examine into the causes of this union of strength and weakness in His will. We shall then see how truly voluntary were His sufferings, and how His very repugnances to suffer were only a new proof of His love for us.

When the Eternal Word took upon Himself the nature of man, He united it to Himself, with all its powers, feelings, and impulses. The brain thought, and the imagination drew pictures; above all, the mighty will did not lose the prerogative of its inherent liberty. Over all this peopled world of thought and desire, the Divine Person ruled supreme; but it was not with a tyrannical sway, or by a blind fatality, that He wielded the powers of His new nature. He violated none of the laws which He Himself had set, and respected its very freedom. As a man cannot be said to guide or rule his will, as though it were a possession, but is so entwined and made one with it, that its every movement is himself acting, and its very freedom is the spontaneous stir of his inmost being, so the Everlasting Son moved and acted in His human will. He did not force or absorb it into Himself; it lost nothing necessary to its perfection, and furthermore its native operations were unimpaired by the Word who exercised them. At the same time, though it lost no right, it gained inestimable privileges. The sons of Adam are vacillating between good and evil; but no angel's will was ever fixed on the Eternal Good with half the tenacity of the human Heart of Jesus. Each wildness and waywardness of passion was forever laid to sleep; no desire could rise unbidden, to mar the harmony of the whole; and the perfect nature answered like an instrument of music to the touch of the Lord, who had made it all His own.

Such was the glorious state of the Humanity of Jesus, with all the dignity of freedom, yet without the power of sinning. It was therefore by a free act of both His natures that the Eternal Word undertook to become the victim for man. Most fearful indeed was the weight which He took upon Himself. What a world it was into which its God had ventured! What a scene was that which broke upon the consciousness of the Sacred Humanity when it first awoke to life! The world had fallen, and ever since its fall a dreadful debt had been accumulating day by day, and hour by hour. The blood of Abel, and the pride of the first conqueror, and the lusts of the cities of the plain, were but the prelude and the type of what was to cry from heaven for vengeance. All this was to be expiated and atoned for; and the second Person of the ever-blessed Trinity had come down to take it on Himself. There was no time for trial, no possibility of probation; and all at once the Eternal Word, with the full spring of His conscious human will, bore up the mighty load.

Let us never forget then how free and voluntary was the sacrifice of the Sacred Humanity. It would have been contrary to the conditions

of the compact by which the Divine Son was
substituted for guilty man, if He had offered up
a forced and reluctant will. A perfect victim
must be free and unrestrained. It was no fatality of its birth, or blind instinct of its nature,
which urged on the human will of Jesus. No
inexorable law* compelled the Eternal Word
to die for guilty man; and therefore without
involving any sin in His Manhood, He might
have avoided death. Inevitable, indeed, it was
for the human nature to follow the Divine Person; but it was only as a man chooses with his
own free will, that the Son of God made His
election through His human will. A perfect
Manhood had been prepared for Him; and He
used it to suffer and to merit with. If it had
been a blind, unwilling slave, the merit would
have ceased at once. If it had been dragged
after Him as an irrational victim, the atone-
ment would have been imperfect indeed. Therefore it was with the conscious voice of His inmost Heart that Jesus cried out: "Lo! I am
come to do Thy will, O God!" The intellect

---

* It is not necessary to pursue farther a question, which
perhaps is the most vexed in theology. It is sufficient to point
out that these words are intended to express De Lugo's view
De Incar., Disp. 26, Sect. 8.

understood the vast plan of redemption; it grasped the needs of man, and heard the cries of souls in danger of falling into the everlasting pit; it comprehended the extent and the horror of the debt contracted by the guilt of man. Then on the other hand, simultaneously, and without succession, came upon it the thought of the dishonor done to God; and with the clear view of all that He was to suffer, filled with the desire of avenging God and of saving man, the Eternal Word substituted Himself for the wretched race. With one act of strong volition, He rose to meet the awful weight; and all in a moment, without the rush of impetuosity, or the strain of effort, the earthly will freely and voluntarily, unmoved but not immovable, upbore it all. He looked abroad upon the earth, and saw "that truth had been forgotten, and that good men lay open to be a prey. He saw, and it appeared evil in His eyes, because there was no judgment. And He saw that there is not a man; and He stood astonished because there is none to oppose Himself: and His own arm brought salvation to Him, and His own justice supported Him. He put on justice as a breastplate, and a helmet of salvation upon His Head; He put on the garments of vengeance, and was clad with zeal as with a cloak."

Up to this time we have seen nothing like weakness; all that we have witnessed is a human will drawing from its union with the Godhead a strength not only unconquered, but unconquerable.

But there are some everlasting laws of God which time cannot alter, which are more unvarying than nature, since no miracle ever comes to disturb them; and one of these is, that a victim must, by the very force of the term, undergo suffering. There was to be one more solemn time in which He was to exhibit Himself before the world in this awful character; it was the time of His Passion. From the first instant of His conception He had looked forward to this moment. He desired to pay the ransom for men, and to open for them the gates of heaven; there was a fire of love shut up in His heart, which was a very pain to Him till it could find a vent in outward suffering; and He longed for His baptism of blood. And now the time is come, and, like a poor victim, He advances into the garden of Gethsemane, to be tied to His willing stake. You know that when God sends any one down to earth on a mission for His glory, He furnishes him thoroughly with all that is necessary to play his part. On He came then, every limb of His beautiful body, from head to foot, filled with more than human sensitiveness, every nerve surcharged with delicate feeling, ready to be bared for the sharp instruments of God's awful justice. Yet behold, at the very moment when all is ready, when heaven and earth are waiting in solemn silence for the spectacle, before an enemy has come in sight, or a hand been raised against Him, the mighty Victim falters and trembles. As the shades of evening close around Him, by the light of that paschal moon, His disciples gaze in wonder upon pallid features and a sinking frame, and they listen in astonishment to that voice which had often awed multitudes into silence, now sunk to its gentlest accents, and proclaiming that His soul was sorrowful even unto death.

Oh! miserable race of man! is the only Heart which has loved thee as yet with untiring and unconquerable love about to grow faithless, and desert thee at the last? Or is the will of Jesus subject to caprice or change, that now, when the chalice which He had longed for was close to His lips, He puts it aside like a wayward child? But no, it was for the very purpose of embittering the cup, and of making it more human, that, out of His love for man, by an act of His sovereign will, He bade these terrors come over His soul.

Let us never forget that the soul of Jesus, as well as His body, was precisely the same as that of other men, except that it had never possessed the power of sinning; and even this it would have possessed if it had not been assumed by the person of the Eternal Word.* His was simply a human nature, undestroyed by its union with the Godhead. Therefore, besides the strong, indomitable will naturally in league with, and perfectly obedient to the reason, it had all that lower nature of feeling and emotion, which stirs the human heart in spite of will and reason both. Let any one try to analyze for himself the varied elements of which his being is composed, he will find a vast world of thoughts and feelings within him so little in his own power, that outward things are able to call them forth when he would wish them most away. Let but the proper objects come before us, and all at once indignation, hope, or fear,

---

* Of course grace might confer the privilege of sinlessness, as in the case of our Lady.

agitate the soul which but a moment before was calm and tranquil as a child. Oh! what a nature is ours, trembling alive to every impulse from without, like some wondrous instrument in the hands of a viewless spirit, touching the keys, and evoking what sound he will! It is as though the feelings were the links which bind body and soul together, partaking of them both, passive and impressible as sense, yet once set in motion, gifted with all the activity of spirit; and all the while the reasonable soul sits upon its throne within, and trembles at these strange impulses, which, like some subtle essence, thrill through its inmost frame, and make it quiver. They are the very stuff and matter of which human passions are made; they are the clamorous parts of poor humanity, which make themselves heard and felt, while the voice of the unseen will and intellect within can scarce be heard; and some of them there are of such a dreadful power, that though the soul recoils at their very loathsomeness, yet there is not a being on earth but would yield to them without the grace of God. Now, as for these last, it would be blasphemy to suppose that the very shadow of them could affect the Heart of Jesus. But what an awful power of moral suffering is there in the heart of man, even short of that inflicted by sin! what elements of weakness are there in it, without even the semblance of guilt! It is the very plaything of terror and shame, of hope and fear, which agitate it by turns, and arise naturally within it, whenever the fitting object appears before it; and even short of these sources of suffering which may be dignified with the name of passions, what a number of feelings are there which chill and unman it in its most courageous moods, and stop it in the full career of its loftiest enterprises. Sinking of heart and weariness, disgust and repugnance, low spirits and despondency, all these are the real miseries and weaknesses of human nature. Unreasonable as they are, they outweigh the strongest arguments; involuntary as they may be, they wear out in time the most indomitable will. When they are away, martyrdom is an easy task, but it is a sudden panic which disperses an army of heroes. It is with these that the sinner and the saint have equally to contend; it is these which make temptation strong, while they unnerve the soul. Yet it is with these, that while hell is raging round Him, and heaven's wrath presses hard upon Him, the soul of Jesus has now to contend. It was by no involuntary instinct that He suffered them, for His soul differs from ours in this, that it was perfectly under His control. What a saint, in spite of himself, feels, but resists by the power of his will, the Heart of Jesus never felt at all without His own consent. Never would they have dared to rise up within Him if His sovereign will had not given them leave; but He now gives the word, and all at once His soul, which a moment before was lying in majestic calm, seems stirred from its very depths by a mighty tempest.

No wonder, then, that all at once, as you watch His figure wandering among the silent olive-trees, He falls down with His forehead pressed to the very earth, like a man with a burden on him heavier than he could bear. No wonder that the Victim, who has upon Him the sins of a whole world, should lie crushed beneath the weight. It required nothing less than a superhuman power to uphold it; and He has stripped Himself of all sensible strength, and therefore, the mighty warrior at once lies prostrate on the ground. You might think that He was dead if it were not that the audible beating of His Heart proclaims the agony which goes on within Him. No need of the

help of demons to paint upon His imagination
scenes of guilt and horror; He had but to turn
His inward eye upon what He knew of all the
sin that had been, and was then, and was to be
till the day of judgment, and the knowledge
of the dread reality was quite enough to break
His loving Heart. There lay the mystery of
sin called up before a soul that could take it in;
and we have seen already how it bowed Him
to the ground.

But there is still a lower depth in the sufferings of that Heart which we have not entered yet. We have seen how the strength of His love made Him suffer; and there was enough already to make His soul sorrowful unto death, when lo! another tempest comes across it. His face grows paler still, and His limbs are trembling. But a moment before His heart was filled with joy at the thought that He could die for them; but now, like an army from hell, there came upon His soul the thought of all the suffering that His passion would involve. Now it is that the hopes of demons revive; they had watched Him round to find a vulnerable part on which they could exercise their skill, but now at length He fears. Oh! could He not in mercy have spared Himself this passion at least, the most imperious and overwhelming of all? As long as a brave man can look unappalled upon torture and death, he can bid his enemies defiance. Even disgrace is powerless over the man who can bear up under it; but when once he is unmanned by fear, he bids farewell at once to dignity and honor. Yet this is the feeling which takes possession of the soul of Jesus, and bends it hither and thither like a reed shaken by the wind. Visions of His awful passion come crowding on His soul, and scare Him with wild affright. Is He to give His body to His enemies to do their very worst upon, when a single word would bring millions of angels to His side to drive the fiends away? The dreadful judgment, the dark visages of His foes, and the sentence of death, all rise before Him. He foresees the blows and spitting on His face, and all the while His inmost soul is filled with unutterable repugnance, and He shrinks with disgust from the thought, as a modest maiden would shrink from contact with an insulting crowd. And then deeper in the night another scene appears; the very dignity of manhood is gone from Him, and in shame and nakedness He stands, tied to a pillar, while His virgin flesh is torn to strips by the awful scourge. Then, farther on, a mighty crowd is deliberating on His fate as He stands before them, with the crown of thorns around His matted hair, tearing His temples, while the blood is filling up His hollow eyes, and pouring down His cheeks. And the crowd sways to and fro with contending passions; till looks of savage hate converge upon Him, and the wild yell, "Crucify Him, Crucify Him," rings in His ears. He turns in horror from the scene, but the demons press upon Him still. "Think not to die yet," they cry; "the worst is yet to come." The poor suffering Manhood must be crushed to earth under the heavy Cross, and die a thousand deaths, while the Godhead keeps it still alive to suffer. And worse than all, His mother's eyes are there, piercing His breaking heart with her speechless agony; for she too must suffer with Him, and not a blow can reach His soul but through her virgin bosom; and she must hear the nails crash through His hands and feet, and see the tortured frame stretched living on the framework of the Cross.

His agony redoubles at the sight, and while His human soul cowers with fear, and seems to the demon's eyes to reel and quiver at the thought of His mother's grief, then it was that He thought anew how useless would be His sufferings for so many of the guilty race of man. After all, how poor would be His triumph! when He was dead and gone to heaven, what uphill work for His religion! a miracle is wanted to convert the world, and a fresh one to keep His faith alive to the world's end, so careless would they be of the precious treasures which He had died to give them. Was it worth while to die to send on earth a sword, to tear families asunder, and rend the strongest ties? And the demons promised Him bloody persecutions for His own, and trials too great for flesh and blood to bear, while visions rose upon His soul of Laurence on his bed of flames, and virgin bodies torn with whips, and honored matrons dragged before inhuman crowds, all for His name's sake. He saw the weak ones falling from Him, because the trial was so sore. He looked forward to the time when the world would call itself Christian; yet even then, everywhere, to the day of doom, the same miserable scene comes before Him, truth all but dying out, and heresy triumphant, whole kingdoms sold and bartered for miserable interests, for lust, or gold, or power, the good men cowardly, and the bad men brave; and all the while His own dear little ones beguiled and wandering without a shepherd, His mother's name blasphemed, and His sacraments trodden under foot. And then there lay beyond the awful world of heathenism. Entire generations are to be swept from the earth before they hear His name, or worse than all, whole nations are to hear it to curse the day when Christian men came near to teach them vices which they never knew before, or else to make of them hereditary ministers to avarice and sin. And was it for such a world as this that He was going to die? An awful repugnance rose within Him, as again there came before His inmost soul the thought of man's ingratitude, and how many would be lost in spite of all His sufferings. He looked for those who should stand foremost in the battle with Him. He turns His sickening eye upon the gulf. Oh, horror! some are there struggling in the grasp of demons, ghastly shapes, with a priestly character. Some are His very spouses, whom He had wedded to Himself. Nay, even the sight of the mass of Christians in a state of grace, adds poignancy to His agony. What He expected was a burning love of God, and

He found it feebly struggling with the love of self. What He wished for was compassion with Himself and with His blessed mother, but He saw His sufferings forgotten, or remembered, as men think on dead relations, whom they have never seen, and whose benefits they enjoy. He gave them grace enough, with Seraph's love, to follow Him to the cross; He looked to them to share His glorious shame, but He found them shunning Him because His brow was blood-stained, and His cheek was pale, though it was all for them. He looked for His very apostles to be at His side, as once they were when His face was serene and beautiful, and divine power flowed out from His very robe, and crowds hung upon His words; but where are they now who boasted that they would die with Him? The very sight of the first blood drawn in the deadly fight has frightened these brave men away. The very shadow of the soldier-band by moonlight, and the rustling of the leaves beneath their steps, has made them vanish from His side. What wonder, if with all these tempests rolling over Him, the soul of Jesus is tossed to and fro; poignant grief smites His frame; blank terror scares Him; repugnance and despondency lie a dead weight upon His soul; and there rises up from the bosom of the earth His cry of agony, "Father, if it be Thy will, let this cup pass from Me; nevertheless, let not My will, but Thine be done."

Oh! most mysterious words! yet it cannot be that the will of Jesus is overcome at last, and that He would give up His Passion if He could. It needed not that suppliant tone if He had wished to shrink from dying. No command from heaven that would have made it sin, or that He could not avoid, was laid upon Him. He could have prayed His heavenly Father, and legions of Angels would have been sent to help Him. No! that prayer was but the cry of His lower nature, which bears witness to the truth that He is human still. It is the voice of His Sacred Heart, which would have us know the struggle which went on within Him, and how He vanquished in it. All the while that the tempest beats upon the surface of His soul, the indomitable will, down far below, is calm and undisturbed, and the final resolve to die for the suffering race is all unmoved. But see, the bleeding Heart can bear no more, and the cold beads of sweat upon His brow are turned to blood, and fall in crimson drops upon the ground.

Oh! awful witness of His sufferings and His love! No scourge has touched His flesh, no thorn has pierced His brow, or nail His hands, and lo! the Sacred Heart sends out its Precious Blood. The silent stream wells forth, to show how, with spontaneous love, the Heart of Jesus longs to die for man. Ah! royal Heart of Jesus, noble in Thy strength, most noble in Thy weakness. Who will dare now complain how hard it is for flesh and blood to fight against itself, and tread the weary path of perfection, since Jesus suffered His own flesh to shrink? and while, with uncomplaining, unresisting meekness, it obeyed the leading of the will, yet still its trembling and its blood bore witness to the contest which is felt within. Blessed for evermore be He who was so far in love with poor humanity, that He must needs embrace its very weakness, and bend His giant strength to sink beneath its woes. He knew that there were inward griefs which gnaw the heart of man worse than the gibbet and the rack. There is a power of grief in human hearts of which the angels can know nothing. Insult, and shame, and unrequited love, affections rudely torn, and foul ingratitude, can wound, and make it bleed far more than outward pain can rend the limbs; and there are times when separation, or neglect, or rude abandonment, can crush the bleeding heart, and turn its whole capacity of loving into a source of poignant grief. And yet, O royal Heart of Jesus! Thou wouldst sound the utmost depth of bitterness which human hearts can feel. If Thou hadst come unmoved and firm amidst the storms of grief, we might have said that Thou wert but some high ideal, far above what we might hope to follow. If we had seen Thee bear Thy Passion, with a brow serene and calm, we might have worshipped and adored the majesty of grief, and turned away without a hope of ever treading in Thy steps. But when we see Thee with pallid face, and lying on the ground, we recognise the tenderness and weakness of a love like a mother's. Each of the throbs that send the gushing blood through every pore betrays the mighty agony of love which struggles in Thy heart. The strong emotions which shake Thy frame show that Thou art human still, and we cheerfully take up the cross to follow Thee. Blessed art Thou who thus canst canonize the very weakness of the human breast, and frame the matter of a sacrifice out of the varying moods of our feelings. Blessed art Thou, for after Thine example even we dare to offer to God the very weariness of mortal life, discouragements and repugnances to good, the flagging spirit and the despondent mind. And when the trial is too sore for our weary hearts, and we all but feel inclined to give up the very wish for saintliness, as though it were a dream, oh! what a joy it is to turn to Jesus, and implore Him, by the trembling of His Sacred Heart, to help us in our utmost need to drag with an indomitable will the fainting spirit on, though it should cost us blood.

Such, then, is the spirit of the devotion to the Sacred Heart, a spirit of unbounded confidence in Him, which makes us cling to Him at the very moment when the conscious shame of our cowardice would drive us away. It bids us look out of ourselves upon Him. There was a time when, high in hopes and filled with noble resolves, we threw ourselves upon the spiritual life, determined to do great things for God; and now that the bitter lesson of our own weakness would make us well-nigh despair, we turn to the Heart of Jesus and hide ourselves there, well knowing that our only hope is in the pure love of Him, who loved us first, un lovely as we were, and will love us to the close, in spite of weakness and imperfection.

Happy they who serve a God of such boundless and forbearing charity! Priests, whom He daily feeds with His most precious Blood, holy religious, whom He has wedded to Himself in the quiet of the cloister, devout souls who are serving Him in the world, happy are you, for He has loved you with surpassing love. You are they for whom "His soul labored," the bright spots on which His agonizing spirit loved to dwell. It was your names that the Angel whispered to Him, to comfort Him in His agony, when He arose and calmly met the drawn swords and lanterns, which flashed with ruddy light through the darkness of the garden, proclaiming His tormentors near. He thought of you in the odious embrace of the traitor; it made the scourge fall light, and the thorny crown sit easy on His brow; the cross ceased to gall His shoulder, and the nails no longer tore His hands and feet, when His dying eye descried you from the summit of His cross, through the lapse of ages. And when you came into the world, and your wayward soul was taken with the fleeting loveliness of creatures, and you left your Creator and Redeemer, with what a yearning eye of love He followed you in your mad career! What mighty powers He put in force to win the wanderer back! The thunderbolts of heaven fell thick around you, not to annihilate the guilty wretch, but to drive you back like a cowering creature to your only refuge. The Holy Ghost, in accents of tenderest love came pealing forth in your inmost heart the loud calls of God's mercy, to bid you come back to the Father, who loved you still; while angels brought bright flashes of illuminating grace from beneath the very throne of God, and Mary's pleading eyes gently reproached you with your black ingratitude. And when at last some efficacious stroke of the mercy of heaven came down at the right time and place, and won the wanderer back at last, with what joy did the Good Shepherd welcome you to the Sacred Heart, the home which you had left.

Let us never quit this house of refuge, and we shall be safe; let this be our house and our abiding place forever. "Put me as a seal upon thy heart, for love is strong as death;

the lamps thereof are fire and flames. Many waters cannot quench charity, neither can the floods drown it." And if we fear lest our own coward will should separate us from Him, let us remember the words of Jesus to His servant, when she complained that her will had not strength enough to make a sacrifice, which He asked of her. "Put it," He said, "into the wound of my Sacred Heart, and it will draw from thence power enough to overcome itself." "Oh! my God," she answered, "do Thou put it there so deep, and shut it up so close, that it may never go out more."

CHAPTER VI.

THE HEART OF JESUS IN THE BLESSED SACRAMENT.

WHENEVER any being upon earth confers a benefit upon us, the first thought of our minds is immediately, What can we do for him in return? This is the natural instinct which God has implanted in our souls. No matter how slight the benefit is, the human heart expands, like a delicate flower, to a smile or a look of affection, and feels grateful even for the sympathy which heals the wound caused in it by a rude word or a gesture of contempt. In accordance with this instinct of our souls, what can we do for Jesus? We can save our souls, it is true, but while we are doing our best to do so, our heart all the while cries out within us, what can we do for Him? The Sacred Heart of Jesus will answer the question for us. Jesus is at the right hand of God, but "this commandment that He commands thee is not above thee, nor far off from thee; nor is it in heaven, that thou shouldst say, Which of us can go up to heaven to bring it unto us? Nor is it beyond the sea, that thou mayest excuse thyself, and say, Which of us can cross the sea and bring it unto us? but the word is very nigh unto thee, in thy mouth, and in thy heart, that thou mayest do it." What He requires of us is, love for love; and, in His infinite mercy, He has chosen to remain on earth with us still, in the Blessed Sacrament, that we might surround Him there with a ritual of love and tenderness dear to His Sacred Heart, as that of the very angels in heaven. It is, above all, to Jesus in the holy Eucharist that the devotion to the Sacred Heart has an especial reference; and as we have entered into the depths of His love toward man, so we will now hear from the lips of our Lord Himself what our love can do for Him in return, as He lies in the tabernacle on the altar.

Many a century had passed over the Church of Christ before there was any distinct feast of the Blessed Sacrament; and when in the thirteenth century our Lord chose that it should be instituted, He had recourse to a holy nun, in a vision, to be the instrument of this devotion in His Church. St. Thomas was living then, and so was St. Louis, but God chose neither the learning of the one, nor the royal power of the other, to be the means of executing His desire. From the age of sixteen, for many years a vision perpetually haunted a young Belgian nun, Juliana of Retinne, whenever she knelt in prayer. A brilliant moon continually appeared before her, with one small portion obscured and invisible. She tried in vain to chase the vision away; at last our Lord Himself came to explain it to her. He said it was to show that the ritual year of the Church was incomplete until the Blessed Sacrament had a day of its own; and He spoke of the aid which the Catholic doctrine would receive from the institution of this festival, at a time when the faith of the world was growing cold, and heresies were rife. Lastly, He bade her announce to the Christian world His will that this feast should be observed. Tremblingly the maiden received the command, and heartily did she pray to be released from the charge. Our Lord answered her that the solemn devotion which He ordered to be observed was to be begun by her, and to be propagated by the poor and lowly. Twenty long years had passed, and her secret still lay in Juliana's breast; she dared reveal it to none, and yet an interior impulse urged her on. So terrible was her repugnance, that she shed tears of blood over it. At length she imparted it to her confessor, and, with her leave, he consulted others. From that time it became a public question, and sorely were men divided upon it. Canons and monks protested against the new devotion, and urged that the daily sacrifice was sufficient to commemorate the love of Jesus in the Blessed Sacrament, without a special day. But the faithful nun prayed on; civil discord raged around her, the city where she lived was lost and won, sacked by a lawless army, and retaken; three successive convents were either burned or otherwise destroyed over her head, yet no earthly troubles could make her forget the task which her Lord had assigned her. She died before it was accomplished; yet she had done enough in her lifetime to provide for its execution. In her wanderings she had met with a few men with devotion to feel, and learning to defend the feast of the Blessed Sacrament. When she was in her grave, the sovereign Pontiff wrote to inform one of her companions, that he himself had celbrated the feast with the cardinals in the holy city. The triumph of the Blessed Sacrament was complete; St. Thomas Aquinas composed its office; the devotion spread through the length and breadth of Europe. From that time to this every Church in a Catholic country, from the cathedral of the royal city to the village chapel, keeps the festival. The procession issues into the streets, followed by the authorities of the realm; it is the public recognition, by the Catholic world, of Jesus in the blessed Sacrament. The prophetic eye of our Lord saw in futurity this very doctrine attacked, and the faith in sore danger. In the full career of the victory of His Church, in the zenith of its medieval splendor, He foresaw our times. Surely no omen* was ever better fulfilled than that which promised the Church good service by the institution of Corpus Christi day. In France it has survived every revolution; its re-establishment has ever been the measure of the Church's power, and the proof of her re-

---

* In one of the visions which occurs in the life of the B. Juliana, one of her companions saw the saints in heaven praying, "Ut nunc tandem aliquando ad confortandam, confirmandam—que fidem Ecclesiæ militantis navam solemnitatem mundo periclitanti patefacere festinaret." Vita S. Julianæ, apud Bolland, 5 April.

turn. It is the dove with the olive-branch, which proclaims the passing away of the mighty deluge. The memory of the procession in which, when a child, he scattered flowers before the Blessed Sacrament, as it passed through the streets, is a hold on the very libertine, and the pledge of his final conversion. The civil and military pomp displayed is a proof that the country is still Catholic, and the very infidel compelled to pass the Blessed Sacrament bareheaded, or to remain within his house, bears witness to the fact that public opinion is Christian, and to the triumph of the Blessed Sacrament.

Such is one of the victories of Jesus; and it is so complete, that a second of the same kind would be superfluous; but, alas! He has sustained His defeats too. If France has stood steadfast, if the south and centre of Europe are Catholic, England is gone, with the whole of the north. Again, among Catholics themselves is not there coldness in individuals? are there not fruitless and irreverent communions? is there no such thing as sacrilege? Reparation is wanted as well as triumph, and this is provided for by the devotion to the Sacred Heart. This is the secret of its power, and the propelling force of its astonishing propagation. It was told throughout Christendom that Jesus had complained in a vision of the deep and multiplied insults and outrages perpetrated on His Body and Blood in the holy Eucharist, that He had asked for sympathy, and that He would accept a love for His Sacred Heart as a reparation for all those injuries.* The news spread, and confraternities were organized all over the world. Neither sea nor mountain could be an obstacle to the progress of the devotion; it overleaped the boundaries of kingdoms, and the Atlantic was no barrier to its advance. It penetrated into China; it evangelized Canada. The remnant of the Indian race has retired, before civilization, to the Rocky Mountains, and the Sacred Heart has pursued them thither with its love. A Jesuit father has converted a whole tribe of them by calling them after its name; so true is it, that its onward force is as yet unstayed.

Love is impatient and cannot wait, and long before the seal of the Church had been set on

---

* "I require that the first Friday after the Octave of the B. Sacrament should be set apart as a festival in honor of my Heart, to make reparation for all these indignities." Life of Ven. Margaret Mary, i. 211.

the devotion, it had spread far and wide. Christians offered their acts of love with the spontaneous impulse of unreasoning affection. That they could not thus atone for all the insults done to the Blessed Sacrament they knew, for satisfaction weighs and estimates the dignity of the person who offers to atone; and who can expiate an injury done to God? But though the atoning power of love is limited, its influence upon another loving heart is unbounded. Immeasurably high among men as Jesus is, He chooses in His boundless mercy to feel toward the love of His creatures, as though He were their fellow-creature. What He alone has a right to command, He chooses to accept thankfully, as though it were a gift. Injured justice in exacting satisfaction requires an equivalent, and considers the person who pays it; the blood of a peasant cannot wash out the stain on the honour of a king. But love proceeds on other principles. The emperor may be grateful for the love of the meanest subject in his realm, because love in its very nature is the willing fruit of the human soul, which no power on earth can call forth till it has proved its right to it. God alone need not wait to show His title, for it is so deeply engraven in our nature, that it is involved in the very thought of Him, the moment we have reason to master it. Yet in His own deep love for us He acts as though it were valuable to Him, and incomprehensible as it is, the devotion to the Heart of Jesus seems to make it plain and easy to us. He has there proclaimed that His Heart follows the laws of other human hearts, is grateful for affection, is pleased with sympathy, and will accept a poor act of love, as though it were a fitting compensation for the loss of kingdoms.

This, then, is the spirit which should animate the confraternities of the Sacred Heart. Their office is, by their affection to make up to Jesus for the insults of men. He has told us that our acts of love can reach Him even now, and that He will accept them as a reparation for the wrongs which are done to Him, especially in the Blessed Sacrament. It will be necessary, therefore, for us to consider the condition of the Sacred Heart in heaven, and how it is that it can be affected on the one hand by the sins of men, and on the other by our love.

Lift up your eyes to the throne of God, at the right hand of which is Jesus in His glorified Humanity. Go forth, ye daughters of

Sion, and see King Solomon in the diadem, wherewith His mother crowned Him in the day of His espousals, and in the day of the joy of His heart. The time of grief is past, and the day of everlasting joy has appeared in the East. Ecce homo, behold the man. His diadem is no longer the crown of thorns which pierced His temples through; and the face so lately bedabbled with blood, and livid with blows, is now the very beauty of Paradise and the joy of angels. Thanks be to God, no grief can reach Him there; and the eyes which looked through the veil and mist of blood upon a sea of fearful visages below, are now lit up with the everlasting light, and calmly rest on Mary's happy face. As for His Sacred Heart, the fountains of the great deep are broken up within it, and springs of heavenly gladness gush from its inmost recesses. The surging waters of bitterness which overwhelmed it in the Garden of Olives have passed away, but "the floodgates of heaven have opened," and the joys of the beatific vision have overflowed the whole, even down to the lower world of feeling and desire, from which they had been withheld. The very possibility of grief is gone from the soul, as suffering has passed away from the body. Yet in the very midst of the songs of the angels, our childish devotions whispered on earth can find their way to Him; amid the caresses of Mary, an act of love breathed from a human breast can influence His Sacred Heart.

It is true that He cannot mourn, but there are other human feelings besides pain, and fear, and disappointment. There are joy, and love, and mercy, and all that involves no suffering, and these can affect Him by turns. With this thought in our minds we are in a condition to solve the question, as to whether the devotions of Christians can be so childish as to be beneath the notice of Jesus. Remember that He has carried all His affections with Him to heaven; it is of "Jesus Christ, yesterday and to-day, and the same forever," that we are speaking. Look at that beautiful child, playing about the fields of Nazareth. When the Jews saw Him, with His long hair flowing down His shoulders, gathering flowers to bring them to His Mother, they only said, "How beautiful is the son of Joseph and Mary!" and did not suspect that He was their God. And now, the arm which sways the powers above, is the same as that which was often flung round Mary's neck.

Furthermore, to make the parallel complete, at the very moment that He was thus a little child on earth, with His innocent heart feeding in gladness upon the joys of childhood, the intellect which swayed those tiny limbs, and moved that playful hand, was fixed at the same time on the beatific vision, and was filled with the vast knowledge which it possesses now in heaven. No wonder, then, if now that He reigns above, His Sacred Heart is childlike as when He was on earth. No wonder that any act of devotion which we offer Him now that He is in heaven can repair the ingratitude of our fellows, and forms a part of the triumph of His glorified humanity.

Little, indeed, does he know of the Sacred Heart of Jesus Christ, who imagines that because it is in heaven, and insensible to sorrow, it is therefore indifferent to what passes on earth, and is beyond the reach of insult or of reparation. Apply this argument to His Godhead, and you at once become an infidel. How, it might be said, can any thing affect the glory of God in heaven? Supposing that to-morrow's sun never rose upon the world, and that men upon earth, and saints and angels in heaven, were all to return to their primeval nothing ness, would God have met with any loss? He had already passed an eternity alone before they were made, and His happiness has not increased for all their poor six thousand years of life, nor would it be less if He were alone again. Yet, who but an atheist would go on to draw the conclusion that God is indifferent to what passes on earth? By the very fact that God created the world, He has bound up His glory with it. It was His own act and deed; He need not have done it; but once the creatures made, He must stand to them in the relation of Maker, and they to Him in that of the work of His hands.

Now carry this on to the Incarnation; the moment that the Eternal Word assumed human flesh and blood, He by His own act put Himself under His own laws. He came down upon earth and trusted Himself to the hands of His creatures, and when they insulted and scorned Him, He was dishonored. This is true of Him still, now that He is in heaven. He has left His glory in our keeping upon earth; He has identified it with our salvation. When sin is committed, He is dishonored. When souls are put into a state of grace, His glory is increased. Now, therefore, from the right hand of God,

He looks down upon the wondrous scene which meets His eye, where the sacraments are doing their work, and His priests are striving to save souls. Of old, it was whole kingdoms which came into the Church at once, and the Apostles were glad, because it was His name that was honored, and His glory that was spread. And now that He seems to have fixed His eye upon individuals, and to do the work bit by bit, which was once done by wholesale, it is no less His empire that extends itself, and His Sacred Heart which triumphs while these victories of love are gained. He works for any one soul by the energetic operation of His grace, as though He cast His whole kingdom on the die, and thought His crown in heaven would not be worth keeping if that soul were not saved. And this is all true, notwithstanding all that has been said about the supreme and imperturbable joys of the Sacred Manhood in heaven.

Again, what was it to Almighty God, if the whole race of man had got their deserts, and had perished forever after the fall? He would have lived on forever in unutterable joys, unimpaired by the agonies of the guilty race. Nevertheless, He did pity them, and what is more, came down Himself to die for them. It does not follow, then, that being raised high above the possibility of suffering renders God indifferent to the cries of His miserable creatures. It is, therefore, a mere confusion of ideas to suppose that, because the human Heart of Jesus can receive no increase of joy, it is therefore in the least more indifferent to the fate of sinners than when it was on earth.

No, it is not selfish in its joys. Take away the notion of pain or restlessness, His Sacred Heart is as anxious as ever about the salvation of His creatures. The torment and the agony are passed away, but the intense burning love of souls, and desire of their salvation, remain in all their force. His not feeling the torture of this desire is a mere accident; He would even now if He could. The necessity of His state compels Him to forego the suffering. Gladly would He come down to the cross as to a bed of roses, if He could save one sinner more thereby. But what can He do more than He has already done? The merits of His sufferings are already boundless, and how can He add to the Infinite? If He died a thousand deaths He could do no more; **you** cannot add a single unit to what at its very outset was beyond the power of number.

Furthermore, with a prudent foresight, enamored as He was of suffering for souls, between the evening of the Thursday, when the first blood was drawn in the dreadful battle, to the last drops which fell beneath the Cross on Friday afternoon, He continued to crowd into His Passion woes enough to furnish forth an eternity of common suffering. There is no exaggeration in this: alas! the subject-matter admits of none. I am only putting into other words what you will suspect to be the extravagant view of some spiritual writer, but is really the grave sentence of an unenthusiastic theologian.* The grief of Jesus was in one respect greater than that of the damned, and of the very demons of hell. Each of these miserable souls in their everlasting wo pays the penalty of his own sins, neither more nor less; but over the soul of Jesus there hung at once the view of all the impurity and the blasphemy, and all the other sins, which have filled the fiery vault of the dungeon of the damned. That one mighty act of perfect contrition for the united sins of all mankind, as it rose

---

* Dolor Christi pro peccatis hominum excessit in intensione omnes dolores dæmonum vel hominum cujuscunque rationis sint. Suarez, de Incar.. Disp. xxxiii. Sect. 2.

silently from the depths of the Heart of Jesus, was deeper far than the everlasting cry of terrible despair. Each one mourns his own dreadful fate, careless of his fellows' suffering; but Jesus mourned for all. Each one mourns out of his deep despair; but Jesus suffered from a deeper source, from the love of God, and a zeal for His glory; this "love is strong as death," this "jealousy is hard as hell, and the lamps thereof are fire and flames." The death and the funeral of those lost souls were wept with tears of blood in the Garden of Olives. And even now the sight of that deep, unutterable hell, and of His poor children hurrying into it, would be enough to create a new Gethsemane and a new Calvary. The Heart of Jesus has not lost its first love, the love of souls. It brought Him down from heaven, and He has carried it back to heaven with Him again; and even now, through that ever open wound in His side, there bursts forth the flame of love; and we can do Him no greater despite than to suspect that it is colder now amid the joys of heaven than it was on earth.

So much for the present affections of the Sacred Heart; they are not the less real, nor the less intense, because they can cause Him no pain now. Now we will pursue the same thought further, and apply it to His glory. It is no fiction that sin dishonors Him, though He is so far beyond its reach that it cannot make Him suffer. It is true He cannot now feel the shame which it inflicts, yet who would say that sin does not dishonor Him because it does not actually come in contact with Him? It despises His laws under His very eyes; it laughs to scorn His presence. It falls indeed under His inevitable dominion in another way; the sinner glorifies His justice in hell, but that is in spite of himself; he has previously by his sin most really taken away from the glory of Jesus upon earth. Sin is His old enemy; when it caught Him upon earth, it thought to mar His work by crucifying Him. It spat in His face, it struck Him with its fist, it clothed and unclothed Him as it pleased, and then sent Him naked to His cross to die like a slave and a robber. In one word, it dishonored Him. This is what it did to Him when He was on earth; this is what it would do again if it could reach Him, and since His Manhood is beyond its power in heaven, it does its best to tarnish His glory now. Sin narrows the bounds of

His kingdom and defiles the members of His Body. It robs His crucifixion of its fruits. It makes His pains unprofitable and His blood of no avail. It knows well, better than we, perhaps, for it is wise in its generation, what the glory of the Heart of Jesus lies in. It knows well in what He has chosen His honor to consist. He has bound it up with the multitude of His faithful ones, their unity and their love. He has placed it in their purity, their meekness, their humility, devotion, and love of God. His very jewels, whom He has put as the "seal upon His Heart," are the innocent and the pure, young men and maidens, living in chastity. It knows where Jesus has left His heart upon earth, and with a dreadful instinct 't goes straight to it, and pierces it as best it may, by robbing it of its dearest treasures, of that for which His best heart's blood has been shed. It corrupts the faith of Christians with heresy, or it sets them one against another, and makes them quarrel. Wherever it can find purity, it defiles it; wherever it falls in with simplicity, it gives it its own false refinement, and makes it hollow-hearted and unreal as itself. This is its constant work, and in one sense it succeeds.

Though the Heart of Jesus cannot suffer now, yet its work is marred, and its glory upon earth is tarnished.

Furthermore, in one case this dishonor is done to Him, not in the person of others, but directly in His own. Not a year passes but what, in some part of Christendom, a tabernacle is broken open, and the sacred vessel which contains His Body on the altar is carried away, perhaps by the hands of Catholics. You enter some Catholic town, it may be the very centre of Catholicism itself; the Churches are open, the Blessed Sacrament is exposed, and set on high, with numberless lights burning about it. Still it is no time of joy, for crowds come into the sacred edifice with looks of sorrow and repentance. You ask what it means, and you are told that it is a solemn act of reparation for a sacrilege committed in one of the Churches of the holy city. Meanwhile, where lies the stolen Host? Who can tell? On the ground, in some out-of-the-way shed, or about the person of the wretched robber, or it may be used for some demoniacal incantation. Do you call this no dishonor, though all the while Jesus lies calm and unmoved with the beatific vision about and within Him? Do you suppose that the Sacred Presence goes, and that the Body of the Lord, by some means, takes its flight, and is borne away by angels, while the foot of the wretch who has violated its abode treads it into the dust? No, though it be true that pain cannot touch Him, He remains there passively suffering this indignity. This is but a type of the state of the Heart of Jesus in Heaven. It cannot bleed; it is safe from sorrow; it rests in everlasting bliss; it is ineffably glorified in heaven. But it has a glory upon earth too, which fluctuates with the rising or sinking zeal of Christians. It does not suffer, but it is not apathetic. It is tranquil like His very Godhead, but it is not passive. Like His Godhead, it works evermore, even on its day of rest; above all it loves with its old love, like the love which God felt from all eternity, pure, disinterested, untiring, and undiminishing, notwithstanding the ingratitude of man.

If such is the state of the Sacred Heart of Jesus in heaven, there is nothing wonderful in the fact that He deigns to accept the homage of our devotion, and that His Holy Spirit suggests to His Church such devotions as from time to time should be expedient for her children. First and foremost He raised in the hearts of Christians a love for Mary, His Blessed Mother. She shared His griefs and sorrows when they were on earth together, and He left her there behind Him for a time, to carry on the traditions of His Sacred Heart. At last, when the time was come, He took her away. He said to her, "Arise, make haste, my love, my dove, my beautiful one, and come. For winter is now past, the rain is over and gone; let thy voice sound in my ears, for thy voice is sweet, and thy face comely." He placed her by His side, that He might have near Him one with human affections to confer with about His Church. He has crowned her queen of heaven, and He tells us that His Sacred Heart* is wounded for the love of her who is all in all to Him, whom He calls His spouse and His sister, as well as His mother. He speaks to her about the poor souls whom they have left on earth, and He says, "Let us see if the vineyard flourish, if the flowers be ready to bring forth fruits." When the Church is hard pressed without, and the love of Christians waxes cold within, then He lights up in their

---

* Vulnerasti cor meum, soror, mea sponsa.

hearts, through His Holy Spirit, some new devotion to her, and she comes down to save, "as the morning rising, fair as the moon, bright as the sun, terrible as an army set in array." In these times, however, He has given us the best gift of all, the devotion to His Sacred Heart. He has come down to tell us that, after nineteen centuries of sin and ingratitude, He loves us as He did the very day when He died upon the cross. He looked abroad upon the desolate earth, and He saw the wild havoc which sin had made upon it. Of old time, when the newborn race of Adam was sinning in the flower of its strength, He had "been touched inwardly with sorrow of heart," and had brought the waters of a great flood upon the earth, to destroy all life. But when that flood had failed to do its work, and the world had gone back to its sins, He cleansed it with a stream, not of anger, but of love, and bathed it in His precious blood. And now that His very cross is forgotten, and the decrepit earth is sinning on in her dotage, what will He do to show His love? As He looks from heaven on the earth, the same scene of wickedness comes before Him. The moon and the stars look down, as of old, on scenes of sin over hill and vale, and under every green tree, and each vast town, like a seething caldron, still sends the everlasting exhalation of its sin, for incense up to heaven. Then, besides this general view, His eye is forced to gaze upon each particular sin; and the thrice told of innocence seduced is acted in all its dread reality before Him, and for one soul saved, thousands and tens of thousands perish. No wonder if, in the desperation of His love, He weaves a mystic crown of thorns around His Sacred Heart, and surmounts it with a cross, and comes to tell the world that through sin and through ingratitude, through failing faith and freezing charity, it loves on to the end.

And now it is plain what we can do in return. If earth can dishonor Him, it can glorify Him too; if our fellow-men are ungrateful, we can rally round Him, and make up for their shameful betrayal by our love. If He has chosen to speak to us in a tone more of sorrow than of anger, as a friend deeply hurt by the ingratitude of those for whom He has given His all, we can assure Him in return how we sympathize with Him, and with burning acts of love make up to Him for the shame of our fellows. God forbid that we should be so faithless as to withhold these acts of love which He has asked of us on the plea that they are useless, and not worth His acceptance. Though love were of no use beyond itself, who would say that it is profitless?

We cannot, indeed, make restitution to Jesus of the souls which have betrayed Him, but we can redouble our own love, since He tells us that it will please Him, and repair their ingratitude. Does not the caress of an innocent child, as it kisses away her tears, soothe the mother's heart, though it cannot undo the ingratitude of her other children? When a beloved prince has been wounded by the hand of an assassin, and is lying sick upon his bed, his faithful subjects send him assurances of love from every town and city in the realm, to tell him how it grieves them that any traitor should be found among them; and their affection soothes the heart of the prince, even though the blow has been struck, and cannot be undone. Thus when Jesus appeals to Christendom, and tells us how insults worse than death have been offered to Him in the Blessed Sacrament, what more natural, even if He had not told us so, than that we should gather round His tabernacles, and tell Him, with burning love, how we at least would do our little all to repair the injustice?

Away with the faithless thought that our poor acts of love are useless to Jesus. Mary did not reason thus when the agony of Jesus was over, and He was dead. When the Pharisees were gone, and there was the silence of death round the cross, when the darkness rolled away, and the pallid form of the dead Christ met her view, she kept her constant watch at the foot of the cross, though her stay was useless save to show her love. When the centurion transfixed His Sacred Heart with his spear, it was as though her own was pierced through and through, though Jesus felt not the blow, and the insult was impotent. And when they took Him down, and laid the ghastly body in her lap, she kissed the livid lips, and washed every bleeding wound, though her kisses had no object but to show her love. Last of all comes Mary Magdalene to show how great is the value of an act of love. She hovers round the tomb where He is lying, to weep over His body, and to anoint with her sweet spices the corpse of Him from whose living lips she had heard that her precious ointment had soothed His heart, though it fed not the poor, nor clothed the naked, and was an utter waste, save that it was an act of love.

We have Jesus ever with us; He has trusted Himself to us over again in the Blessed Sacrament, notwithstanding the experience of Calvary; and He has met again with the like treatment, sacrilege, and insult, the traitor's lips, and the soldier's taunting jest. He has told us, that to compensate for this, we must receive Him into our own hearts with greater fervour, visit Him in His tabernacles, and make acts of reparation and love to His Sacred Heart. And now, where in the wide world are we to find a place where reparation to Jesus is more needed than in this great city in which we dwell? Here the pomp and pride of Tyre, and the lusts of the cities of the plain, have formed an alliance with the ingratitude of Jerusalem. Three hundred years of insult to the Blessed Sacrament have to be expiated. Not a dome or steeple that rises above the roofs of the city but marks the triumphs of a false creed over the Catholic faith, the expulsion of Jesus from a Catholic altar. Thousands of busy feet pass unconsciously near the lowly chapels where He resides; and the full tide of human life rolls recklessly past the altars where His very Heart is still burning with love. And when the darkness comes on, and He is left alone with the solitary lamp, sin is wakeful still, and prowls around the streets and squares, while He is watching and loving all night long. If grief could reach Him in the Blessed Sacrament, this would be enough to turn every tabernacle into a new Gethsemane. When the wickedness of a great city was once brought in visible shape before the Blessed Mary of Oignies, and she saw a great scandal in the streets, she threw off her shoes, and with a knife which she had about her, cut the soles of her feet. Then with her bleeding feet she walked over the ground where the sinners had trodden, that her blood might wash away from the bosom of the earth the outrage done to its God. It is not blood that Jesus asks of us, but acts of love to His Sacred Heart. And wherever its adoration is extended, and its image honored, He has promised to rain down blessings and graces from Heaven in return. There is a hidden power of intercession in it; and who can tell what conversions might not be wrought through the length and breadth of the land if the anger of God was appeased by frequently offering to Him the love of the

Sacred Heart? Who can calculate how many souls might be nightly saved from temptation if Christians, in their visits to the Blessed Sacrament, or before a picture of the Sacred Heart, said one Hail Mary in its honor, to ask that there might be one mortal sin less committed that night in London?

Oh! do not suppose for a moment that such thoughts are fit only for Priests, as though an ordinary Christian could sit quietly down in the midst of such a city as London, and go about his occupations without taking an interest in the horrid battle which is going on around him. I cannot understand how any Christian can pretend to love God and remain indifferent to the fearful dangers of souls. On the contrary, the Clergy look to the laity for the support of their prayers. There are times when the heart of a priest, battling for God in some great modern city, is ready to fail him. Let him at any given moment realize how the scattered powers of evil gather themselves together upon this one point of God's earth, multitudinous in their attacks, yet concentrated in their energy, subtle enough to penetrate everywhere, yet embracing a mighty field in their operations Let him but consider their awful success in spite of God and God's Church, how the very frame and structure of society seems made for the purpose of neutralizing the Sacraments, and of keeping men by bonds stronger than material ones from the Precious Blood of Jesus. Placed in the very centre of the mighty contest, he can interpret its every move, and see whither it tends; to him each victim is a soul, each blow dealt in the battle has its event in hell. It is a very agony to him to think on the multitude of sins which the moon and stars look down upon in one single night; how, amid the tall squares and labyrinthine streets, the passions come periodically forth, wild and untamed in their onset as a barbarian host, yet with all the perseverance and organized discipline of civilization. Alas! human beings are there, baptized Christians too, it may be Catholics, once innocent and pure, whom some one imprudent step, one single slip of the foot, has precipitated from depth to depth, while society so holds them down, that whenever they attempt to rise, they are sucked down again, till it seems as if the very grace of God could no longer reach them. Oh! when he is thus bewildered by the very noise, confused and dizzy with the multitude and greatness of the interests at stake, ready to die with sickness of heart, and overwhelmed with the danger of precious souls, he feels inclined to cry out, Oh! my God, why all this misery upon Thine earth? why is sin allowed so dreadful, so destructive a power?

It is in such moments as these that it is a joyful thought for a priest that there are good souls fighting against this evil, in the quietness of their homes, by devotions to the Sacred Heart. It was a happy thought to establish in the Cathedral of the Archdiocese of Westminster a Confraternity, the object of which was to make reparation to Jesus for sacrileges and insults offered to Him. The devotion to the Sacred Heart was offered to England when first it arose on earth; it was then treated inhospitably, and banished from the realm. A second time God offers it to us; let us cherish the precious gift. It will produce among us what we want most of all, hearts dwelling on Jesus as a person, as a real being, God and man once on earth, now in heaven. It will enable us to realize the value of souls dear to Jesus. It will teach us the supernatural powers of our religion, and show us how it is the one heavenly thing upon earth, as heavenly now as eighteen hundred years ago, the one representative of Jesus, the one teacher of His truth. Above all, it will teach us to live more and more the life of Jesus on earth, since it will help us to sympathize more and more with His inmost thoughts and feelings. It will reveal to us His burning love, and fill us with love for Him in return. And what can produce this love like devotion to the Sacred Heart? It was there that was concentrated the fire which He longed to kindle on earth. Its very life was love. It was created to give a local habitation and a material shape to the charity of the Eternal Word for His poor creatures. Mary's womb was its birthplace; it sprang from her pure blood; all in a moment it rose within her, the Heart of God, the spring of His human life, charged with His love for man. Its first throb was an act of love; and it went on, through every phase of joy and sadness, bearing the action of this mighty influence till it broke upon the cross.

THE END.

www.ingramcontent.com/pod-product-compliance
Lightning Source LLC
Chambersburg PA
CBHW032112230426
43672CB00009B/1712